HYPNOTHERAPY FOR HEALTH, HARMONY, AND PEAK PERFORMANCE

Expanding the Goals of Psychotherapy

Catherine Walters
Ronald A. Havens

BRUNNER/MAZEL *Publishers* • NEW YORK

Library of Congress Cataloging-in-Publication Data

Walters, Catherine.
Hypnotherapy for health, harmony, and peak performance :
expanding the goals of psychotherapy / Catherine Walters, Ronald A. Havens.
    p.   cm.
Includes bibliographical references and index.
ISBN 0-87630-690-3
1. Hypnotism—Therapeutic use. I. Havens, Ronald A. II. Title.
[DNLM: 1. Hypnosis. WM 415 W235h]
RC495.W33 1993
615.8'512—dc20
DNLM/DLC
for Library of Congress   92-48326
                                                 CIP

Published by
BRUNNER/MAZEL, INC.
19 Union Square West
New York, New York 10003

Manufactured in the United States of America

10 9 8 7 6 5 4 3 2 1

To Larry and Marie with love.

And to our parents,
Joseph and Dolores Walters
and
Arthur and Eleanor Havens.

CONTENTS

Learning to Manage Attention with "Hypnosis"
Pretrance Preparations
Conducting a Hypnosis Session
Summary

PART II: TRANCE SCRIPTS

PREFACE

This book offers a conceptual foundation and instructions for using trance to improve mental and physical health and to increase competence and optimism at work, school, and play. We also explore trance as an avenue to the goals of enhanced pleasure, heightened self-esteem, and inner tranquillity.

The fields of medicine and psychotherapy are shifting slowly but decisively away from the traditional emphasis on pathology toward a concern for wellness and prevention. Increasingly, researchers are discovering that paying attention to what is good and right about our minds and bodies leads to enhanced health and mental well-being, whereas a constant concern with the negative aspects of our physical health, behavior, and emotional life may be hazardous and counterproductive.

The wellness paradigm encompasses a variety of conditions frequently overlooked or underplayed in traditional approaches to health. Individual uniqueness, the indivisible wholeness of mind and body, and the healing aspects of sensual pleasure, contact with nature, physical activity, humor, and creativity are all facets of the concept of wellness. Intellectual stimulation and meaningful relationships also appear to be necessary for optimal health, as are work satisfaction, a robust optimism, and spiritual contentment.

Although most of us would affirm the value of these conditions, we would be hard pressed to find an introductory medical or psychotherapy text that encourages their creation. Such books almost invariably concentrate on how to diagnose and "cure" the perceived causes of problems. To some extent our previous book, *Hypnotherapy Scripts: A Neo-Ericksonian Approach to Persuasive Healing* (Havens & Walters, 1989b), conformed to this tradition. In it we explored the use of Ericksonian hypnotic techniques to locate sources of psychological and physical pain and to facilitate the natural healing powers of the individual. In the present text, we present a broader, more holistic application of hypnosis. We expand the healing emphasis of our approach to incorporate the new paradigms of wellness, higher consciousness, and optimal performance. We suggest that trance can be used just as effectively to promote joy and harmony as it can to quiet disharmony. We also suggest that the promotion of well-being often is a more efficient and beneficial focus of attention for psychotherapy and hypnotherapy than is a constant concern with diagnosis and cure. Thus, in writing this book we turn to less traditional sources for our conceptual foundation. We refer to literature on mental and physical wellness, mind/body connections, peak performance in sports and other settings, states of consciousness, and attention.

Our review of the relevant literature and our clinical experiences with trance lead us to the following conclusions.

1. There are specific, identifiable thoughts, actions, and experiences that create well-being and peak performance.
2. These internal and external events are available to everyone but not everyone pays attention to them or takes advantage of them.
3. Hypnotic trance is an effective way to direct attention toward these events.

In Part I of this book we discuss the implications of incorporating the ingredients necessary for wellness, peak performance, and spiritual tranquillity into the practice of hypnotherapy. We examine the role of conscious attention in human experience and discuss the use of hypnosis to captivate and redirect attention toward desirable states of mind. We also offer guidelines for eliciting trance states and explain how to compose a sequence of trance experiences that encourage participants to move toward their individual goals.

In Part II the reader will find scripts of actual trance sessions that exemplify our basic recommendations regarding the hypnotic process. These scripts demonstrate how to use hypnosis to capture attention and focus it in ways that nourish wellness, promote contentment, support optimal performance, or precipitate peak experiences. They employ metaphors, stories, and direct and indirect suggestions. They incorporate a variety of poetic allusions, as well as puns, rhymes, mythic symbols, and entrancing rhythms. All seek to expand self-awareness, self-expression, and self-mastery. We believe this expansion is the key to lifelong well-being.

We do not suggest that the approach described within these pages is the only path to harnessing inner resources. The meditative practices of Zen and yoga, for example, represent traditional means to similar ends. We find trance to be useful because of its remarkable flexibility and adaptability. As a path to self-awareness, it conforms to the needs and interests of almost everyone. As a path to wellness, it provides a direct route. Before we can adjust our course in life, we must be able to pay attention to the relevant landmarks. Trance directs attention to these landmarks, and it provides a pleasant trip as well.

ACKNOWLEDGMENTS

We are indebted to the many people who contributed to this book. First, we want to thank Marie Havens and Larry Shiner for using their editorial skills so diplomatically throughout its many revisions. Never have so few read so much so many times! In the reading and useful comments department, we also wish to thank Kathlyn Abbott and Theresa Eytalis for their excellent feedback.

Sangamon State University students Kathy Crietzberg, Nina Dexter, Wade Frazier, and Larry Rogers researched the literature on attention for us during the early stages of this book. John Miller also graciously provided copies of research materials related to our interests. And then there is Jackie Wright, who typed our references faster than a speeding bullet. Thanks to each of you.

Of course, a very special thanks is due Natalie Gilman, Editorial Vice President of Brunner/Mazel, for her encouragement, guidance, and flexibility. She offered enthusiastic support for our ideas, tolerated our decision to revise our original format completely, ignored the lateness of our final manuscript, and had a baby in less time than it took us to write this book. Congratulations, Natalie, and thanks.

We also are grateful to the many professionals who wrote to us after reading our previous book. Their generous praise let us know that our writing was useful to their work and it spurred us on as we wrote this book.

This book was written in several states, as well as states of mind. We are indebted to Victor and Juliet Brudney for the use of their home in Cambridge, Mass., while we worked at the Harvard University Library. Thanks also to Kay and Richard Klausmeyer for their support during work at the University of Arizona library in Tucson.

In addition to those we both want to thank, there are certain people we would like to acknowledge separately.

Ron would like to thank:

The Psychology Program faculty members at Sangamon State University for their consideration while I worked on this manuscript. Being able to work undisturbed at my computer for hours on end helped immensely.

Sangamon State University, for honoring me with the Distinguished Service Award, which funded student workers for this project.

Michael and Daniel, who have been a rewarding source of inspiration, learning, and joy for many years.

Cathy gives special thanks to:

Kathy Abbott, to whom I especially want to express my affection and respect. Kathy's humor and insights were invaluable. (And I'm sorry I made her go to Tennessee!)

Laura Field, whose seminal work at the University of Texas on exercise behavior and wellness provoked so many great discussions and assured me I was on the right path.

Deborah Evans, Candy Cates, and the fitness staff at Lake Austin Resort, for inviting me to present several workshops on wellness and pleasure. My work for them was instrumental in the development of this book.

And to Sister Pauline Lorch, the first person to tell me about the healing benefits of hypnotherapy—thanks, wherever she is.

PART I

Concepts and Instructions

1

ENHANCING LIVES

The important thing is to get the patient to do the
things that are very, very good for him.
(Milton H. Erickson
in Zeig, 1980, p. 195)

During the first several years of our professional practices, we
received many calls from people who ordinarily do not consult psychotherapists. These individuals contacted us because they knew
we were using hypnosis therapeutically. They did not have problems to solve, but simply wanted to know whether they could use
hypnosis to enhance their existing potentials and skills. A successful fashion designer, for example, requested hypnosis to stimulate
her creativity. Bright and successful students sought hypnosis to
absorb information more readily and to improve their test-taking
skills. Weightlifters, golfers, and runners wondered whether hypnosis might give them the extra "edge" needed to move beyond
their current level of performance. Physicians, psychologists, real
estate agents, accountants, and attorneys desired that same edge
for taking their licensing exams. Ministers, spiritual seekers, and
those interested in meditation sought to deepen their experience
of mindfulness and to become more solidly and continuously at one
with themselves and the world. These clients were eager to use
hypnosis to experience greater happiness, to achieve peak performance, or to heighten creativity. However, unlike our psychotherapy clients, they did not perceive themselves as troubled or
lacking in contentment. Rather, their goals for themselves centered on *increasing* the skills, confidence, and contentment *they
already possessed.*

Initially, we were a bit surprised, even put off by such requests. Most therapists are trained to deal with emotional or psychological difficulties, but here were clients who were far from troubled. What they wanted was more of the "good things" in life. At first, we tended to treat our sessions with these clients lightly, viewing them as entertaining breaks from our "real" work. Yet, the more we worked with such individuals, the more we realized that our ideas about what constituted "serious" reasons to consult a therapist were derived from a model that emphasizes the elimination of pain and problems rather than the promotion of health and happiness. Although it will always be important to assist those who are in pain, it finally occurred to us that we should also give serious attention to maintaining and enhancing the lives of those who are still healthy. Therapists have much to offer, and to learn from, this segment of the population.

Our most startling realization during this conceptual transformation was that the hypnotherapeutic procedures we were developing to enrich already happy lives were equally effective with those who were unhappy or even miserable. In fact, our "serious" therapy clients responded quite enthusiastically as we incorporated these procedures into our approach. They welcomed the opportunity to discover how to feel good about themselves and how to have fun with their hypnotic abilities. We learned that even a successful search for solutions or complete relief from discomfort can be disappointing if the client is not also provided with the compensatory experiences needed to foster a highly positive sense of self. Furthermore, removing a source of pain, depression, or anxiety does not automatically produce pleasure, joy, or contentment. It merely leaves people in a neutral condition.

On the other hand, as increased optimism and contentment become the focus of therapeutic intervention, not only do we induce healing, but we also feed a sense of self-esteem and purpose. In many instances, positive therapeutic change may occur without concentrating on the nature and source of negative thoughts or feelings at all. When people have the ability to experience joy and then suddenly receive permission to surrender themselves to that experience, depression and anxiety can be rapidly displaced.

Much as we might like to believe that we developed these understandings on our own, the fact is that they are a direct reflection of the position emphasized throughout the writings and lectures of Milton H. Erickson, M.D. Erickson emphasized the future, not the past, and focused on the positive instead of the negative. Our experiences with our clients allowed us more fully to appreciate this fundamental aspect of Erickson's work.

ERICKSON PROMOTED WELL-BEING

Although known primarily for his innovative approach to hypnosis, Erickson was also a remarkably insightful and creative psychotherapist. In fact, his hypnotherapeutic and psychotherapeutic procedures often were so creative that they confounded his colleagues. Erickson's interventions may have seemed atypical and confusing to other practitioners because they were based on personal observations and clinical experiences rather than on one of the traditional personality theories. Erickson rejected what he called the "procrustean bed of theory"and relied, instead, on his own unique way of looking at things.

Erickson's perspective represented a revolutionary paradigm for the therapy process (cf. Havens, 1985a). Rather than using therapy to identify and cure problems, he concentrated on thrusting his patients into positive, life-enhancing experiences. Erickson emphasized the existing skills and abilities of his patients, not their disabilities. He redirected their attitudes and behaviors toward positive ways of being and did not concern himself very often with the how or why of their preexisting unhealthy attitudes and behaviors (cf. Zeig & Geary, 1990). This perspective represented a radical departure from the operating principles of most therapists and physicians at the time, who were firmly committed to the notion that the goal of therapy, like that of medicine, is to locate and eradicate sources of pathology. Erickson located and created sources of wellness.

For example, years before it was empirically determined that altruistic acts are psychologically and physiologically beneficial, Erickson routinely gave his patients altruistic assignments. He once instructed a socially withdrawn and depressed 52-year-old woman, who enjoyed raising African violets, to begin propagating numerous cuttings from her plants and giving them to members of her church. From then on, whenever there was a christening, wedding, or funeral, she was there with her gift. This kept her occupied and happy for the next 20 years. As Erickson described it, "Anybody that takes care of 200 violets is too busy to be depressed" (Zeig, 1980, p. 286). He got her to do something that would make her feel better instead of trying to figure out why she was depressed.

Similarly, Erickson sent depressed men off to dig gardens for others, gave some clients pets to care for, and, in general, got his patients involved in activities or experiences that produce positive feelings and attitudes. He arranged for "accidental" meetings between patients that resulted in happy marriages and improved lives. He had "losers" sign up for college classes and social isolates take dance lessons. He helped one young girl experience the thrill of victory by challenging her to a bicycle race. He did not talk about "curing" people. Instead, he talked about getting people to do things that are good for them.

Erickson's rejection of a focus on client pathology is reflected in his writings and in his clinical work. Several years ago, we reported the results of a study in which we located and classified the terms Erickson used to describe his patients in his numerous journal articles and lectures (Havens & Walters, 1986). Of the 153 case presentations we reviewed, we found that Erickson employed no diagnostic terms at all in over three fourths (119) of them. In these presentations he used only common, everyday adjectives to describe his patients.

Thus, Erickson's unique therapeutic approach included both a promotion of enhancing thoughts or activities and a minimization of diagnostic or pathological labeling. Apparently he did not think about his patients so much in terms of their disorders as in terms of their potential for being happy and well adjusted in the future. He then helped them to achieve those goals, often without ever exploring the actual nature or origin of the presenting problem itself. From his point of view, "emphasis should be placed more on what the patient does in the present and will do in the future than upon a mere understanding of why some long-past event occurred" (Erickson, 1954, p. 127).

RESEARCH SUPPORTS ERICKSON'S APPROACH

Erickson's followers have described and analyzed his work in detail (e.g., Haley, 1973; Lankton & Lankton, 1983; O'Hanlon, 1987); published transcripts of his lectures and hypnotherapy sessions (e.g., Erickson & Rossi, 1979, 1981; Haley, 1985; Zeig, 1980); collected examples of his interventions (e.g., O'Hanlon & Hexum, 1990; Rosen, 1982); organized and summarized his comments on different topics (e.g., Havens, 1985b); offered extensive explanations of his basic hypnotherapeutic procedures and principles (e.g., Gilligan, 1987); and gathered all of his journal articles into one set of books (Rossi, 1980)— but until recently, few empirical studies actually tested his approach. The main reason for this is that the dominant, pathology-oriented models of psychotherapy have kept researchers' attention focused on issues of psychopathology. Research on the identification, etiology, or elimination of "illness" has little or no bearing on an approach such as Erickson's, which deemphasizes pathology and concentrates on the promotion of well-being. To illustrate this point, it can be noted that the diagnostic manual of the American Psychiatric Association (1987) acknowledges that the meaning ascribed to events can precipitate or exacerbate virtually any illness, but it does not even suggest the possibility that different attitudes might actually prevent or alleviate illness and promote health. Traditionally, researchers and professionals have concentrated on the negative, ignoring the positive altogether. But this situation has now changed, thanks in large part to a significant paradigmatic shift in the fields of medicine and psychology, a shift toward *wellness*.

Like Erickson, proponents of this new paradigm concentrate on the factors responsible for wellness and life enhancement and avoid the negative consequences of a focus on diagnostic labeling and pathology. The wellness model stresses the positive interactions of mind and body and the healing power that lies within each individual. There are many parallels between Erickson's approach and the wellness paradigm. It is conceivable, even probable, that Erickson's teachings set the stage for the emergence of this new perspective. In fact, one of the first scholarly efforts to identify the mind/body connection in an empirically defensible manner was written by one of Erickson's most prominent students (i.e., Rossi, 1986). Whether or not there is a causal relationship between the two movements, the fact remains that the development of the wellness paradigm revealed an entirely new set of issues for medical and psychological researchers to investigate, and the resulting data provide empirical support not only for the basic tenets of the wellness paradigm, but for Erickson's approach as well.

Research into the basic tenets of the wellness model emphasizes the invigorating consequences of optimistic beliefs and attitudes, the benefits of friendly social relationships, and the value of healthy environmental conditions (for reviews see Kabat-Zinn, 1990; Ornstein & Sobel, 1987; Rossi, 1986; Taylor, 1989). This research also indicates that psychological and physical healing often occur when attention is directed toward humor, mastery, and pleasure, and away from illness. According to Williams, Kinney, and Falbo (1989), an optimistic sense of self-efficacy is the overriding predictor of therapeutic change for those experiencing agoraphobia. What and how we think can even improve our basic immune system responses (Rider, Achterberg, Lawlis, Goven, Toledo, & Butler, 1990). In fact, the wellness literature intimates that we can enhance virtually every aspect of our being by concentrating on appropriate thoughts, actions, and experiences.

Articles and books examining the consequences of various altered states of consciousness, such as "mindfulness" and "meditation," also have extended our appreciation of the intimate, and potentially beneficial, relationship between the mind and body. Research in this field clearly demonstrates that certain states of consciousness offer long-term physiological and psychological benefits (e.g., Benson, 1975; Tart & Deikman, 1991; Wallace & Benson, 1972). In addition, research regarding performance in sports, work, and educational settings has indicated that positive attitudes and specific states of attention promote peak performance, as well as peak physical and mental health. For example, Mahoney, Gabriel, and Perkins (1987) examined exceptional athletes and determined that their concentration and self-confidence tend to be quite high. Similarly, Rich and Woolever (1988) found improved test-taking performance when attention and positive expectancy were increased. What is good for us in one area of our lives turns out to be good for us in many others as well.

Support for Erickson's therapeutic approach also can be found in the literature regarding the factors responsible for personal growth and positive change. Frank (1963) was one of the first to suggest that therapeutic change in all settings, including such seemingly divergent procedures as modern psychotherapy and the healing rituals of primitive societies, can be attributed to the same general factors. He proposed that altruistic acts, hope, emotional arousal, and experiences of personal mastery play a dominant role in the healing process. Like Frank, Yalom (1975) postulated that the trappings of the many schools of psychotherapy (the techniques, theoretical constructs, and specialized language) play only a minor role in producing therapeutic outcomes. To demonstrate this point, he examined and isolated the generic factors responsible for change in many different types of encounter and therapy groups. Yalom's resulting list of beneficial attitudes, experiences, and actions overlaps and clarifies the curative factors emphasized by Frank, by the wellness movement, and by Erickson. It includes altruism, optimistic expectations, a sense of belonging, mastery of new socializing techniques, feedback from others, emotional arousal, a resolution of existential/spiritual issues, and basic information about oneself and the world.

Thus the research from many disparate areas converges on the same conclusion and provides straightforward support for the basic principles Erickson recognized and began using many years ago. This research indicates that such factors as optimism, friendships, doing good deeds, a sense of personal accomplishment, and a focus on the pleasurable aspects of life are the wellsprings of health and competence. These factors are not merely a means to a therapeutic end, but are themselves the desired outcomes of therapy. They are not beneficial because they help to cure problems in some mysterious manner, but because they transform lives into a state of well-being, thus replacing the conditions that gave rise to the problems in the first place.

It may be concluded, therefore, that when the desired outcome is health, the initiation of healthy attitudes and behaviors may be more beneficial than attempts to uncover and cure illness. When the goal is joy, it may be wise to ignore existing sadness and to direct attention toward joyful ideas, activities, and events. As a rule, people will be happier, healthier, and more competent if they do things that are associated with happiness, health, and competence, rather than trying *not* to do things that are associated with unhappiness, illness, and failure. It is much easier to go straight toward the goal from where you are than to retrace your steps in an effort to find out what went wrong and then undo it. The shortest distance between two points *is* a straight line.

The wellness model does not claim that traditional medicine or psychotherapy has failed, and neither did Erickson. Many people are alive today thanks to immunization and antibiotics. And many clients report significant gains as a result of various traditional psychotherapeutic interventions. The pathology-based approaches are so effective at times that the negative consequences of this orientation are rarely challenged (cf. Callahan, 1990). As a consequence, we know a lot about diagnosing problems and a little about "fixing" people, but we do not know much about mobilizing psychological hardiness or inducing feelings of optimism, competence, and control. Both the wellness paradigm and the Ericksonian approach challenge the merits of an emphasis on *fixing* things and suggest that an emphasis on *enhancing* things is more enlightening and more beneficial.

We now focus less on the diagnosis and treatment of problems in our hypnotherapeutic practices and concentrate instead on the creation of the conditions necessary for psychological and physical health, sensory pleasures, inner harmony, and a sense of mastery. Although we still use hypnosis to track down and eliminate sources of emotional or physiological pain when they are distracting the client from more positive pursuits, we now emphasize its use for mental, physical, and emotional well-being. We do so because such an approach takes clients directly to where they want to go and need to be.

WELL-BEING IS AVAILABLE TO ANYONE

Mental, physical, and emotional well-being are often treated as separate phenomena. Nonetheless, they are actually highly interrelated. For example, the conditions necessary for enhanced mental well-being include an expanding emotional calm and a growing sense of physical prowess. Similarly, in order to attain peak performance, we must adopt some of the attitudes responsible for physical wellness and have a strong sense of inner peace. The pursuit of one necessarily involves the pursuit of the others. The interconnected unity or harmony of mind, body, and behavior permanently connects these goals together. If one area of our existence is ignored, each of the others is weakened as well.

The wellness paradigm assumes the interrelationship and reverberating interactions of the body/mind. It also emphasizes process over product and event over outcome, and it respects every individual's unique accomplishments. For example, people may wish to attain total spiritual enlightenment, but few lead lives compatible with reaching this lofty goal. Still, any movement toward enlightenment is valuable, even if the tranquillity attained is less intense than that of a Zen monk living in an isolated temple. Likewise, we may admire the lithe, graceful bodies and amazing physical abilities of Olympic athletes or professional dancers, but the fact that we cannot emulate them does not lessen our delight when we move our own bodies in dance and exercise. Wellness, tranquillity, and peak performance are not about competitive goals and comparison. Rather, the focus is on enjoyment, self-acceptance, and the pleasure of action itself.

People can move toward positive states of mind and action even when faced with what might seem to be severe physical, mental, or situational difficulties. They do not have to succumb to self-doubts, fears, or the application of demeaning diagnostic labels. Whatever their age or accomplishments in life, all people can immerse themselves in the attitudes and experiences associated with well-being. Dr. Erickson provides a prime example. He was color-blind, arrhythmic, tone-deaf, dyslexic, and partially paralyzed as the result of a bout with polio during which he almost died. Later in life, following a recurrence of the polio, he experienced chronic severe pain, was forced to use a wheelchair, and lost much of the strength in his arms and hands. Nonetheless, he maintained a zest for life, a remarkable sense of humor, a genuine interest in others, and a dedication to teaching his unusual therapeutic insights and hypnotic skills. He viewed hardships as necessary "roughage," and once, toward the end of his life, he commented to his students, "Why not live and enjoy, because you can wake up dead" (Zeig, 1980, p. 269). Apparently, Erickson did just that; he enjoyed life and used it to its fullest.

This capacity to enjoy life in spite of hardships also is reflected in a story told by one of the authors (R.H.). He relates the following.

At the age of 12, I spent several weeks in the children's wing of the Methodist Hospital in Columbus, Ohio, recovering from surgery on my dislocated left elbow. I awoke from the anesthesia aware only of a huge weight on my chest. It turned out to be a plaster cast that ran from my hand up to my shoulder.

After several minutes, I began to remember where I was and why. I was in a large room full of beds. At the far end of the ward were three huge iron lungs. I found out later that each held a teenage boy paralyzed from polio. Another teenager, the size of a 6-year-old, lay shriveled and almost paralyzed in a metal crib nearby. Across from me were two other boys, each of whom spent six hours twice a day lying on a rack that rocked him up and down, up and down. They did not require iron lungs, but they did need the mechanical assistance of this rocking to facilitate their breathing. Next to me was a boy my age who was recovering from surgery on his stomach. He was the first to speak to me. He told me all about the other boys on the ward. It took me a few minutes to realize that he was retarded.

At first I was shocked by the entire situation. Then I was scared. This scene was beyond my range of experience or understanding. I had not imagined that such problems existed. Over time, however, I began to enjoy the place. The boys had a sense of humor and fun that also was beyond my experience or understanding. I was used to being bored unless I was doing something exciting or unique. But they could change a daily sponge bath into a frolic that even the nurses seemed to enjoy. They told jokes and made up puns endlessly. They played practical jokes every day, on each other and on the hospital staff. Each had a special interest, passion actually. For most, it was baseball. Jerry, for example, could recite the batting averages and other statistics of every player on the Cleveland Indians. Tim, on the other hand, was always absorbed in a game of solitaire. His goal was to win five games in a row without cheating.

But these boys did not just play. They also worked very hard. They all worked at their physical therapy exercises with an intensity and sense of purpose one might expect from athletes training for the Olympics. They celebrated their accomplishments with the same enthusiasm and joy you see on the winners' platform of any sport. If someone walked an inch further than he had before or lifted an arm higher, it was a major event.

At first they ignored me and went on with their routines, but after a few days I was incorporated into their circle. Even though I would leave soon and they would not, I was included. We had fun. These children knew how to enjoy life more than any of my "healthy" friends outside the hospital did. Most could barely move, but they were never bored. They marveled at the tastes of the food, they discussed the merits of the perfumes the nurses wore that day, they held wheelchair races in the halls. At night, in the dark, they talked honestly and frankly about their conditions. They knew, each of them, what possibilities the future held in store. They confessed their sadness about their situations. They consoled each other and offered support and encouragement to anyone who was feeling low. But they refused, positively and resolutely, to let anything get in their way. As John, the 14-year-old who was so small that he lived in a crib, announced one evening, "Well, I ain't gonna be here long, but I'm sure gonna have one hell of a good time while I am." He did, and he made life rewarding for those around him.

It was a bittersweet time. I made, and then lost, several very special friends. Within three days, two of my new friends were moved to the critical care unit. I later heard that John had died. I still do not know what happened to Terry. I learned how loss feels. I also learned that anyone can be bored, sad, depressed, or scared. Life makes that easy sometimes. With a special effort, however, my new friends took charge of their thoughts and feelings; they stayed on the path of emotional contentment, physical and mental challenge, and spiritual fulfillment. They did this in spite of the traumas of the past, the discomforts of the present, and the dangers of the future. They enjoyed every moment and used every ability they possessed. They loved each other and were a family for each other. When one of them left or died, they mourned his loss and celebrated his life. When I left, I cried, they cried, and then we thanked each other. I have never met a group of people who were more honest, creative, exuberant, self-assured, and playful.

People who are moving along this path have a charm that attracts and frightens at the same time. They captivate with their boisterous spontaneity and startle with their honesty. They entice us with their apparent ease and tease us with their apparent wisdom. They show us that life can be an exciting and rewarding experience, no matter the difficulties. They are whole and free. As such, they provide an example of the possibilities and a challenge to join them on their journey.

Everyone is capable of adopting the attitudes and behaviors that lead toward wellness. We also believe that the experience of peak performance is within each individual's reach and that inner tranquillity is a good place to start rather than end. The common ingredients needed to nurture these outcomes have been identified by various researchers and all are readily available. The scripts presented in Part II of this book were created to evoke the nutrients essential to the development of wellness, tranquillity, and peak performance (optimism, altruism, participation in sensory and esthetic pleasures, etc.). These key ingredients exist within us all, patiently waiting to be summoned and utilized to produce well-being in every area of our lives.

A FOCUS ON WELL-BEING HAS MANY ADVANTAGES

When psychotherapy and hypnotherapy are expanded to include a focus on the ingredients necessary for wellness, peak performance, and tranquillity, several benefits result. First, this broader perspective offers therapy clients a more comfortable way of looking at themselves than is available when a psychopathology-based model is used. Rather than being forced to examine their personality faults and emotional scars, clients are encouraged to focus on their assets and talents. They are allowed to see themselves in a flattering light, to feel empowered, and to operate with the expectation of success.

Second, therapeutic goals are expanded. Instead of concentrating on the problem/patient with the hope of finding a cure, the time and energy can be used to help each client create powerfully positive states of mind and a strong sense of physical well-being. Joy, competence, and increased attention to the right and good things in the client's life become desirable and feasible outcomes. Pain may motivate people to enter therapy, but few are content just to achieve a transitory freedom from discomfort. Becoming a survivor certainly is better than being a victim, but becoming a celebrant of life seems to us to be an even better outcome. Everyone wants to be successful. We want to feel good about who we are. We want to have fun. Simply stated, most people wish to become "weller than well." As our therapeutic model moves toward the positive expectancy of wellness, mastery, and tranquillity, becoming "weller than well" does not seem an unreasonable quest at all. It even begins to sound like the only goal worth pursuing.

This expanded definition of the goals and concepts of hypnotherapy also extends the applicability of hypnosis beyond the confines of the therapy office. It makes hypnosis a legitimate, potentially useful experience for virtually everyone in every setting, not just for those with problems or complaints. For many years professional hypnotherapists have accepted the notion that hypnosis should be used primarily as a "therapeutic tool" with "patients." A vast majority of the professional books and journal articles about hypnosis deal only with its use in the treatment of various psychological, behavioral, and physical disorders. Indeed, Wall (1991) goes so far as to equate hypnosis with the provision of "psychotherapy or treatment" (p. 74). This narrow point of view overlooks the promise of hypnosis as a way to maximize mental and physical functioning. It is wasteful and inappropriate to restrict the use of this procedure solely to people in need of cures and solutions. We might just as well restrict the use of sharp objects to the operating room, eliminating knives, scissors, saws, razor blades, and hoes from our everyday lives.

Hypnosis alone cannot increase the strength of our minds or muscles, but it can enable us to use what we have more powerfully.

As Erickson noted, "Hypnosis cannot create new abilities within a person, but it can assist in a greater and better utilization of abilities already possessed . . ." (Erickson, 1970, in Rossi, 1980, Vol. IV, p. 54). Hypnosis also offers an effective way to inoculate people against the scourges of self-doubt, depression, and anxiety—a way not merely to treat problems once they develop, but to prevent their development. The same could be said for various physical illnesses (cf. Rossi, 1986). Both children and adults might be healthier and happier if they were taught how to use hypnosis to emphasize the attitudes and behaviors that research indicates are directly responsible for psychological and physical wellness.

Along similar lines, the use of hypnosis merely to fix problems overlooks research showing that it also can be used to precipitate peak experiences and other forms of enlightened consciousness (e.g., Havens, 1982). Such studies indicate that hypnosis can produce experiences that lead toward inner peace, feelings of oneness or universal connectedness, and an appreciative reverence for the perfect harmony of our environment.

When the underlying perspectives and goals of hypnotherapy are expanded to incorporate the attitudes and experiences that lead to wellness, peak performance, and tranquillity, hypnosis is transformed from a therapeutic scalpel or a parlor game into a portal leading toward personal fulfillment and self-mastery in all aspects of life, including education, business, and recreation. Hypnotic trance becomes a skill that, like reading, can open new worlds, new understandings, and new ways of being.

Accordingly, this book is written with two primary goals in mind.

1. We hope to encourage, and perhaps accelerate, what seems to be the inevitable and mutually beneficial integration of hypnosis with wellness, altered states of consciousness, and peak performance. We wish to point out that the concepts underlying these fields are appropriate and useful additions to any hypnotherapeutic practice, and that hypnosis itself is

a useful addition to the professional practices of most physicians, counselors, educators, and psychotherapists.

2. More important, perhaps, we wish to make the spread of the use of hypnosis as easy and inevitable as possible. We hope to inspire more professionals to begin teaching more people how to use their hypnotic capacities for their own personal comfort and benefit. To facilitate that end, our discussion of the underlying concepts and basic procedures of hypnosis is as simple, thorough, and practical as we could make it. In addition, we provide examples, with brief introductory discussions and explanations, of scripts that demonstrate how hypnosis can be used to promote the different attributes and experiences associated with wellness, tranquillity, and peak performance.

SUMMARY

Traditionally, the practice of psychotherapy and hypnotherapy has involved the identification and removal of psychological problems and ignored the enhancement of abilities, pleasures, and contentment. As medical and psychological research expands into the area of mind/body relationships, it becomes increasingly apparent that such a limited focus can be counterproductive. Focusing on problems and discomforts leads, at best, to a neutral outcome. More important, however, it distracts attention away from an awareness of those aspects of life that are positive and healthy.

Recent advances in the fields of wellness, peak mental and physical performance, personal growth, and altered states of consciousness suggest that certain changes in attitudes and behavior can be highly pleasant and productive. Other research suggests that the consequences of such alterations can be beneficial whether or not people have problems at the time. This implies that a large segment of the population, in addition to traditional therapy clients, could benefit from experiences designed to promote such alterations.

When the practice of hypnotherapy is expanded to incorporate the goals and perspectives common to the fields of wellness, performance, and spiritual development, the attention of both the hypnotherapist and the client is automatically redirected toward the production of well-being and away from a focus on pathology. This makes the hypnotherapeutic process more enjoyable, perhaps more effective, and certainly more widely applicable.

2

USING ATTENTION SKILLFULLY

> In the process of living, the price of survival is
> eternal vigilance and the willingness to learn. The
> sooner one becomes aware of realities and the
> sooner one adjusts to them, the quicker is the
> process of adjustment and the happier the
> experience of living.
>
> (Milton H. Erickson, 1962
> in Rossi, 1980, Vol. IV, p. 514)

Just because we can identify the raw materials necessary for the
construction of well-being does not mean that we have completed
the job. Baskets do not weave themselves and neither does well-
being. The raw materials have to be gathered, prepared, and
woven together with precision and artistry. A weaver must devote
a great deal of attention to this process in order to produce a
decent rug or basket. All of the mental and physical activities
involved must be carefully monitored and coordinated. The same
applies to the development of well-being—the components must
be gathered and woven together skillfully.

If we wish to redirect lives toward wellness, tranquillity, or
peak performance, to help others weave well-being, *we must learn
how to help others redirect their attention toward the factors
responsible for these conditions*. The perceptions, thoughts, and
actions associated with well-being cannot become a part of everyday experience unless attention is focused on them.

ATTENTION ORCHESTRATES EXPERIENCE
AND ACTION

At first glance, this emphasis on the importance of *attention* may seem a bit puzzling or misplaced. Attention is not a sophisticated notion, but is such a constant and automatic aspect of our existence that we take it for granted. As Goleman and Davidson (1979) observe, "Attention determines what we notice, but we seldom notice attention itself" (p. x).

This is not surprising. After all, we have been instructed since childhood to "pay attention," and we believe that we know how to do so. Unfortunately, few of us were taught how to manage our attention in an effective manner. We were not even taught what attention is or what skills actually are involved in paying attention.

Eastern cultures, on the other hand, have recognized the importance of attention for centuries. Both the Japanese and the Tibetans, for example, have an ancient maxim to the effect that without training, the mind jumps about frantically, like a group of wild monkeys chattering in the treetops. In these cultures, virtually every activity, from throwing pots to the practice of swordsmanship and archery, is preceded by some type of attention-centering ritual (Herrigel, 1971). Meditational practices, yoga exercises, and even the traditional tea ceremony offer an opportunity to calm the mind and to direct attention in a purposeful, focused manner.

This emphasis in the East on the intentional creation of calm, centered states of absorbed attention can be attributed to Buddhism, the dominant philosophy of the region for 2500 years. In his statement of the Four Noble Truths, Buddha acknowledged the relationship between attention and all other aspects of life. He encouraged his followers to attain the *right mindfulness, right conduct, right livelihood,* and *right concentration* necessary for inner peace and for harmony among thought, word, and deed (Conze, 1975). He explained that cravings, fears, false beliefs, and self-consciousness typically distract attention from these goals and so must be eliminated from awareness if thought and performance are to take place in the natural or "right" manner. Finally, Buddha pointed out that those distractions could be eliminated by renouncing all desires and, more important, by learning how to control attention through the careful practice of mindfulness or meditation (Watts, 1957). Small wonder, then, that Fromm (1979) described Buddhism as essentially a theory of cognition based on a recognition of the important relationships between attention and perception, attention and thought, and attention and emotion. As we shall see, this ancient Eastern view of attention was a sophisticated portent of current understandings.

By comparison, Western civilizations did not take notice of attention as an important life skill until very recently. Although it is possible to find discussions of attention in writings dating back to the Golden Age of the Greeks (cf. Norman, 1969) and in the manuscripts of several early Christian mystics (cf. Progoff, 1957; St. John of the Cross, 1953), it was not a topic of serious conversation in our culture until William James (1890) emphasized it in his pioneering text *Principles of Psychology*. Even so, attention did not begin to receive significant scientific consideration for another 60 years—until the 1950s (for reviews see Egeth & Bevan, 1973; LaBerge, 1991).

Research conducted since the 1950s has led experts in several fields to suggest that appropriately directed and resolutely focused attention is the foundation for excellence and goal achievement in most endeavors (cf. Klatzky, 1984; Keele, 1973; Norman, 1969; Warm, 1984). The mastery of complex physical or mental skills and enthusiastic participation in the activities of everyday life depend on effectively directed attention. Redding (1990) found that participation in attentional skills training improves decision-making and problem-solving skills. Boostrom (1992) describes the ability to focus attention as the basic building block of creative and critical thinking. As Buddha indicated centuries ago, many of our accomplishments and pleasures, as well as most of our difficulties, can be traced to our use of attention. Who we think we are, what we believe we know, what we imagine we feel, what we decide to do, and how well we do it, all reflect the contents of attention over time.

Moreover, research indicates that impaired attention management may be the basis for severe mental disorders. Perls (1947) was one of the first to suggest that all disordered behavior is a reflection of gaps or distortions in awareness caused by mismanaged attention. More recently, Maher (1966, 1983) speculated that the symptoms of schizophrenia may be the result of deficits in the ability to maintain and shift attention. Holmes (1991) discussed the "excessive broadening of attention" typical of schizophrenia and related it to a variety of the symptoms associated with this disorder. In a similar vein, Lovaas, Koegel, and Schreibman (1979) attributed the perseveration and withdrawal of autism to "overselective attention," attention that is too narrowly focused. Csikszentmihalyi (1978) stated flatly that the inability to focus attention voluntarily produces psychopathology.

Although there is still much to learn, current knowledge consistently supports the ancient observation that attention plays a crucial, perhaps central, role in experience and behavior.

ATTENTION DETERMINES CONSCIOUS AWARENESS

We are continuously bombarded by millions of sensory and cognitive signals competing for our awareness. Attention is the selection process that determines which of these competing stimuli enter our conscious awareness and which do not (James, 1890).

Generally speaking, attention is directed by specific "policies" or criteria (Ornstein, 1989). First and foremost, we notice events that relate to our safety and physical well-being. We also pay attention to novel events. Meanwhile, we ignore sameness and overlook signals we judge to be irrelevant to our basic needs or beliefs.

Attentional discrimination reduces huge amounts of information to a manageable size. This process, of course, is tremendously useful, but it has its downside as well. Because the parameters of attentional selectivity are often quite narrow, we can miss a lot of worthwhile information.

Information we overlook does not simply vanish. Many of the events that get screened out of conscious awareness still are perceived and reacted to by some parts of the brain (Anooshian, 1989; Broadbent, 1958; Cowan, 1988). As Fodor (1983) and Gazzaniga (1983) point out, the brain consists of numerous modules or "miniminds," some of which operate separately from those involved in conscious awareness. These nonconscious miniminds represent the multiple types of intelligence and countless mental abilities that Erickson referred to collectively as the "unconscious mind" (cf. Havens & Walters, 1989b).

Events that are not noticed consciously may register in one or more of these modules and be analyzed and reacted to there. Furthermore, each of these modules may itself be a source of information or action that typically is overlooked by conscious awareness, either because its output is difficult to perceive or because the policies governing attention direct our conscious awareness away from this output. The result is that we actually know much more than we think we know, and we often do things without knowing it. We may "absentmindedly" scratch an itch while engrossed in listening to a lecture without consciously realizing what we have done or why. The answer to a problem or a forgotten name is suddenly thrust into awareness, a gift from the unconscious. Thus while we may not be consciously aware of an event in our internal mental world or in the external physical world, that does not mean that it will have no effect. Rather, the effect it has is one that we are not ordinarily able consciously to monitor or control.

Conscious awareness, however, is within our grasp. The fact that we have been unaware of many things in the past, including the resources and abilities of our unconscious miniminds, does not mean that it is not possible or desirable to become aware of them in the future. As Erickson said, "The ideal person would be one who had a readiness to accept the interchange between conscious and unconscious" (Erickson, Rossi, & Rossi, 1976, p. 258). To accomplish this feat, we must learn how to manage attention so that we are in charge of it, rather than its being in charge of us.

MANY FACTORS INFLUENCE ATTENTIONAL SELECTIVITY

As one might suspect, learning to manage attention is easier said than done. Even under the best of circumstances, attention is difficult to manage. The focus of attention, and hence the content of conscious awareness, is directed by many variables other than our current choices and preferences. The stability of attention, or the length of time something stays in conscious awareness, also typically is undisciplined and out of our control. The contents and stability of attention can be managed intentionally, but more often than not attention is directed by biased beliefs, unconscious decisions, or attention-capturing external events.

For example, attentional focus is automatically drawn toward any internal or external stimulus that is especially strong or that suddenly changes position or intensity (Broadbent, 1958). External happenings—such as loud noises, bright flashes, and sudden movements—capture our attention no matter what we are doing at the time. Novel events may hold our attention briefly, but as the newness wears off, we become bored and find it difficult to continue focusing on them. Repetitive and confusing things are hard to attend to at all. In addition, various physiological events (such as pain, thirst, hunger, sexual desires, pleasure, itching, warmth, and coolness) can dominate awareness entirely if they become intense enough. For example, it is difficult to attend to a lecture when one is hungry or the room is unbearably hot. The same holds true for emotional reactions such as fear and anger. Extreme emotions can dominate attention and block out an awareness of rational thoughts or physical sensations. An angry person may punch a hole in a wall without thinking about the cost of repair or noticing the resulting broken bones and cuts until later, after the attention-capturing emotion subsides. It takes a great deal of practice to learn how to override such automatic attention-directing responses, responses that alter the content of attention in ways that may or may not be desirable.

Many aspects of modern culture complicate efforts to direct attention skillfully. In general, our world is noisier, more crowded, and more diverse than the world of our ancestors. We simply have more distractions with which to contend. In order to compete with all of these distractions of modern life, media experts conduct sophisticated research to determine how to design radio and television advertisements, billboards, and packages that will stand out and grab our attention. As a result, we are inundated daily with the bright, complex, rapid-fire images and sounds that this research indicates will capture our attention. The overall noise level increases and the next wave of ads becomes even more intense.

As this suggests, some sources of distraction or captivation are a natural result of a more complex culture. Many of them, however, are a result of straightforward efforts to influence both the focal content and the stability of our attention. Advertisers realize that they can influence choices in the marketplace if they can capture and hold attention long enough to direct conscious awareness toward specific ideas and impressions. Parents and teachers also have agendas for the contents of our attention, offering a constant stream of suggestions and directives regarding what is acceptable and what is not. Religious leaders, politicians, and our peers all engage in ongoing efforts to control the direction and content of our attention. Television and movies present us with captivating images of life and the world, which, in turn, influence our awareness of what we are supposed to think is fun, beautiful, exciting, and sexy. In addition, different patterns of reward and punishment are used to alter our tendency to pay attention to some things and to ignore others. We are praised for attending church and ridiculed for listening to the "wrong" music. When people do not develop the skills needed to manage their own attention, they may become captives of those who can. The modern consumer, willing to pay 20 percent interest to purchase an item on credit, seems to be an excellent example.

Thus we are bombarded from childhood on with words and images containing explicit and implicit messages regarding the thoughts, feelings, and perceptions our attention should be directed toward. Some of these attentional directives eventually are internalized in the form of attitudes, values, and beliefs that become the primary content of conscious awareness—that is, the thoughts about ourselves and others that we repeat over and over in our minds and in our conversations. Others just sit in the background, silently altering what we notice.

Other authors have referred to this collection of guiding principles by such terms as the "critical parent," the "superego," the "inner child," and the "conditioned self." We prefer to avoid the complicated theories associated with these terms and refer to a person's guiding principles of awareness simply as the *schemas* or *mental sets* that dominate the conscious mind's focus of attention.

SCHEMAS DOMINATE CONSCIOUS AWARENESS

Bartlett (1932) used the term *schema* to describe the coherent set of rules or themes we derive from our experiences and then impose on the world around us. Schemas are the cognitive structures that predispose an individual to organize and sort incoming information in particular ways (cf. Nesser, 1976; Taylor & Crocker, 1981). They consist of a network of associations and categorizations based on various biases, prejudices, and expectations about the self and the world.

Occasionally, mental sets or schemas are adopted intentionally after considerable thought. But more often, they simply represent the sum of various parental and societal prescriptions for "good" behavior, schemas of shoulds and metaphorical ideals that we use to define ourselves and the world. A few of these schemas remain in conscious awareness, but many sift down into the unconscious regions where they continue to influence or control behavior unimpeded by conscious recognition or desire.

Over time, these prescriptive, often conflicting, schemas accumulate and begin to exert a high degree of control over the nature and content of attention. They become an entrenched set of rules about the way things "should be" and what we "should" or "should not" notice about ourselves and the rest of the world. Schemas generate constant directives and commentaries about everything we notice and all of our responses. Because they are internal and ever-present in the form of thoughts, ideas, and emotional reactions, they often take direct control over attentional selectivity. Attention begins to be focused automatically toward things that are consistent with our schemas.

Even when we do attempt to take charge of attention and direct it ourselves, the choices we make about where to focus it continue to be influenced by the labels and definitions our schemas impose on the world. Our schemas direct us toward events that are consistent with our biased point of view and away from things that are not: "Be careful!" "That's yucky!" "You're stupid!" "This is very bad!" "Don't do that!" "Ignore that!" *Or:* "Enjoy yourself!" "That's good!" "You're smart!" "Look at this!" Whether they tend to be critical or supportive, they bias our view of reality, including our perceptions of ourselves.

These "inner commentators" communicate their biased attitudes and feelings to us continuously. We pay a lot of attention to these messages because they are attention grabbing by nature. That probably is why we adopted them in the first place, and why they continue to influence the way in which we direct attention. They deal with good and bad, right and wrong, and other similarly dramatic evaluations of everything we experience or do. Such messages tend to be either extremely pleasant or extremely unpleasant, and thus attention is automatically drawn toward them. These messages also often contain an indication of powerful negative or positive consequences of our actions. "If you notice this, it will be wonderful." "If you experience that, you will go to hell." Extremely painful or pleasing messages and directives are difficult to ignore, especially when they contain threats or promises that stimulate intense emotional reactions.

Furthermore, these judgments and evaluations are typically presented to us in the language and linear logic of the left hemisphere of the brain. This makes them seem quite reasonable or rational. The biased attitudes and judgments contained in our schemas are offered to us as appropriate and defensible, no matter how counterproductive they may be. Much as an experienced press agent puts a "positive spin" on even the most ridiculous statement, our schemas are based on rationalizations that make them seem right and proper. As a result, schemas play a prominent, almost dictatorial role in selecting the things we notice. They tell us what to pay attention to, and then they tell us what to think or do about what we have noticed. To the extent that we pay attention to these biased communications, we impose certain meanings on our experience. Our conscious perceptions of our self and our world will conform to the prejudices, desires, expectations, and habits contained in our schemas. More accurate or less prejudicial perspectives are abandoned and become a part of the unconscious mind. Meanwhile, biased attitudes and beliefs continue to determine what we perceive and how we interpret those perceptions.

This tendency to construct reality in the direction of our schemas has been demonstrated in a variety of ways. Hastorf and Cantril (1954) took advantage of a controversy over a Dartmouth–Princeton football game to do so. The game had resulted in several serious injuries and provoked a series of postgame accusations. The researchers chose subjects from Dartmouth and Princeton and showed them a film of the football game in question. Subjects were told to keep track of the number of infractions committed by each team and the seriousness of those infractions. Not surprisingly, the students from each school saw more serious infractions by the other team than by their own. They saw what their biased schemas led them to see.

Svenson (1981) noted similar distortions when drivers were asked to rate their own driving abilities. Automobile drivers who had been responsible for one or more accidents were just as likely as "accident-free" drivers to rate their driving skills as superb. Langer and Roth (1975) demonstrated the effects of conscious bias in a series of experiments on gambling. They discovered that people will make gambling decisions on the basis of beliefs in bogus "skills" or superstitions, even when they know that the statistical probabilities argue for a different decision. For example, when players are allowed to pick a lottery card, they will hold onto it when offered a card they know has a better chance of winning because the previously chosen card is already considered "their" card. Similarly, Hayano (1988) noted that people are willing to believe and act on the notion that thoughts can influence the roll of the dice, even when they know that the process is entirely random. People, it seems, live in a world constructed by their schemas. Their reactions to the world and their descriptions of themselves are a reflection of the self-deceptive contents of these schemas.

There is nothing intrinsically wrong with having schemas or mental sets. Our schemas represent an attempt to simplify information and understandings, to establish a view of ourselves and the world that allows us to operate with some degree of intellectual guidance, self-assurance, and social respectability. Without them, it would be difficult to function in everyday life. We would have no rules or explanations to guide our decisions about what to pay attention to or how to respond to it. As long as our schemas direct us toward useful information, they are a valuable resource. But problems arise when we become stuck in mental ruts and cannot shift away from them when a situation calls for new or different behavior and/or attitudes. Sometimes our ruts even lead us in dangerous or counterproductive directions.

SOME SCHEMAS ARE BENEFICIAL, SOME ARE NOT

Certain types of schematic bias appear to be comforting and beneficial. A disposition toward optimism is associated with emotional stability and physical health (Peterson & Bossio, 1991). Positive self-evaluations are linked to enhanced performance and improved adjustment (Ornstein & Sobel, 1989). When the things we are led to notice about ourselves and others are influenced by a bias toward a "kinder and gentler" evaluation, we are less likely to experience heart disease (Harris, 1989; Williams, 1989). A schema that directs attention in a supportive way toward unusual or bizarre conceptualizations may increase creative problem solving (Adams, 1974; Flesch, 1951), and a tendency to focus on images of ourselves being assertive increases assertiveness (Lazarus, 1984). Given these findings, it is encouraging to learn that most people, especially children, tend to see themselves and the world in fairly positive ways (Taylor, 1989).

On the other hand, the biased messages received by the conscious mind can be so painful or confusing that serious emotional or psychological difficulties result. Depression, self-consciousness, distorted body images, and numerous other problems can be precipitated when the contents of negative schemas overwhelm conscious awareness. For example, Seligman (1990) refers to unipolar depression as the "ultimate form of pessimism" (p. 56), noting that the depressed patient has "a dour picture of . . . self, the world and the future" (p. 57). Melges (1982) suggests that when attention is continually bombarded and directed by concerns about the multitude of things that could go wrong in the future, the result can be generalized anxiety, agoraphobia, or panic attacks. Williams (1989) indicates that a hostile schema of the world, which categorizes most people and events as frustrating or annoying, may contribute to ill health. Mathews, May, Mogg, and Eysenck (1990) report research findings that indicate that people who tend to be highly anxious have a strong bias favoring the search for threatening cues, whether or not they are anxious at the time.

Psychotherapy clients provide daily examples of the painful effects of paying attention to negatively biased schemas. Several years ago, one of the authors (C.W.) worked with a woman who burst into mournful sobs one day as she walked into the office. It turned out that she had just completed an important and highly successful work project. Eager to give her special praise for a job well done, her employer had invited her to lunch and she had accepted. She had, in fact, just come from this celebratory luncheon at which she had received nothing but praise. It may seem hard to reconcile this description of events with her unhappy tears, but her negative interpretation of the situation clarified matters. She was sure that her boss had suggested lunch because he felt that since she was 40 pounds overweight, the only reward somebody like her would find satisfying would be a hearty meal. The fact that he had taken others to lunch under similar circumstances was irrelevant. Given this perspective, the only things she had noticed during the meal were how tight she felt her dress was, how often her boss had commented on the quality of the food in the restaurant, and how embarrassed she was to eat anything in front of him. His compliments on her work and offer of a substantial raise had gone practically unnoticed. This ability to construe such negative meanings from such a pleasant set of circumstances is awe inspiring. Powerful negative schemas can direct attention again and again toward angry and critical self-evaluations, judgmental categorizations, and feelings of shame or hopelessness. Such biases control the direction of attention and embed the individual's conscious mind in limited ways of perceiving, thinking, and doing.

This is not meant to imply that negative world views and devaluing self-talk have no basis in experience. We are not all given the same materials with which to weave the cloth of life. Some people receive incredibly hurtful messages about themselves from others, and sad or tragic things do occur. Taylor (1989) argues that there are several conditions that challenge and, in some cases, eliminate the natural tendency toward positive beliefs and attitudes. Victimizing events, especially in early childhood, lessen the ability to view the world as safe or one's self as good. Tragedy and extreme threat can shatter a belief in personal control and instill a mistrust of the self and others.

Clients' negative schemas are often grounded in victimization and loss. Some of them even may have once served a valuable protective purpose in painful situations (Nesse, 1991). However, this does not preclude people from adopting new, more useful schematic frameworks of optimism and self-esteem. As long as human beings are going to have schemas, it makes sense for therapists selectively to encourage their clients toward ones that are pleasant and useful.

CHANGING SCHEMAS CAN BE DIFFICULT

Human beings are built for change. We are able to change because we have to cope with disaster, survive threats, fight off dangerous aggressors, and adapt to a world where things are always changing. Sometimes we change just for the fun of it or the thrill of it. Finding new ways of doing things and learning how to do something new seem to be as much a part of human life as migration is for many species of birds.

Basic as the change impulse seems to be, however, there are times when certain ways of thinking or certain types of behavior become so rigid and embedded that change, even for the better, may seem practically impossible. All therapists are familiar with the way in which negative schemas and debilitating behavior patterns persistently disrupt or destroy their clients' lives. These clients genuinely wish to change, to be happier, to accomplish their work with more ease and success, but they feel stuck, unable to escape their self-criticism and self-doubt. Indeed, they are stuck in their negative biases, their pessimism, or their lack of imagination. It is the paradox of change that we human beings are at once so flexible and yet able to become so rigid and set in our ways.

In doing therapy, changing negative schemas to positive ones is not always easy. Many clients argue that they would change their basic schemas if they knew how, but that they have no idea of how to accomplish these changes. They have trouble identifying their negative attitudes or beliefs because these attitudes or beliefs are "unconscious," or, if they are able to sort them out, they do not know how to replace them. Try as they might, their negative schemas continue to direct their attention in self-critical or antagonistic ways. Witness, for example, the female client of average body weight who cannot go through a day without torturing herself with thoughts of how fat she is, how unattractive her thighs are, how large she looks in comparison with person X or Y. This client often understands quite well that her body image is not in keeping with her actual size. She may even recognize that her idea of a "perfect" body is a cultural invention/convention. Nonetheless, she finds it difficult or impossible to end her self-critical thoughts and does not believe that she can replace this schema with a more nurturant one. She cannot imagine thinking or acting differently.

Other clients will argue that it would be silly, stupid, crazy, or wrong to alter their beliefs. They feel that they have good reason to believe what they believe, or that they must believe it given what has happened to them in the past, even if their beliefs cause them pain. This is especially the case when a client's schemas stem from a traumatic incident or a series of unpleasant events. Guilt, anger, and superstitions arising from such events are often adopted with the fervent belief that they are justified and/or necessary. Such biases make change difficult. The client who is convinced that she is a bad person because she was raped when she dared to go out wearing a short skirt is a case in point. She "knows" she is immoral and that she deserved what she got as punishment for giving in to her desire to be attractive.

In rare instances, all that is needed for a client to change is an observation by the therapist that certain modes of thought or action might be more helpful than those currently being used by that client. In such cases, the relieved client, seeing the validity of this observation, adopts new patterns. Both the client and the therapist are satisfied.

As most therapists know, however, this is not usually the case. Counterproductive schemas can be quite intransigent. This intransigence may be the basis for the clinical notion that the events responsible for the adoption of these schemas must be located and "dealt with" or "worked through" somehow to uproot them. This traditional regressive therapeutic process does not actually change the past at all, nor does it necessarily alter existing mental sets about those precipitating events. It may help clarify the nature of current self-defeating schemas, but it does not automatically replace them with healthier ones.

Other approaches to psychotherapy, such as cognitive behaviorism, do not center on "working through" past issues. Rather, these approaches require clients to catalogue their negative or "irrational" thoughts and replace them with a set of more objective, "rational" thoughts. In these approaches, clients typically are asked to exchange various negative schemas for neutral (i.e., rational) ones. For example, the belief that it would be terrible if everyone did not like the client is replaced by the attitude that it would be inconvenient if people did not do so, but not terrible.

Tracking down the origins of counterproductive attitudes can be a time-consuming process. Challenging the "rationality" of negative schemas also takes considerable time and energy. Furthermore, as Peterson and Bassio (1991) point out, both dynamic and cognitive therapies seem to assume that the absence of the negative somehow implies the presence of the positive. This, in our experience, is not the case. Challenging or eradicating negative schemas will not automatically produce positive ones. If therapy is to be truly productive, clients eventually must learn how to focus attention in the positive directions of optimism, pleasure, and psychological hardiness.

We prefer the Ericksonian hypnotherapeutic approach over traditional methods because it offers clients a direct but gentle way to replace their old schemas with new, more creatively positive points of view. Trance helps to bypass any conscious resistance to change and offers the participant an opportunity to come to terms with his or her schemas without self-consciousness. With the therapist as a guide, the hypnotic state allows the client to "try out" new, more positive schemas and to direct behavior toward more enjoyable, healthier experiences. Trance allows us to achieve the positive ends associated with traditional therapies (removing negative schemas) by offering clients pleasant alternatives to their negative biases, and it does so in a comparatively gentle, nonconfrontational manner. How and why people developed their negative schemas become irrelevant when they begin to adopt more positive ones during the trance experience. People do not have to understand why they felt bad in order to feel better. Hypnosis allows therapists to give clients permission to become optimistic, to disregard past traumas, and to take care of themselves, without insulting them for holding onto irrational beliefs or forcing them to relive unpleasant experiences. It immerses them in positive experiences and bathes them with a comfortable awareness of cognitive and behavioral alternatives. Changing schemas is difficult, but hypnosis can make it easier.

Whether positive or negative, however, schemas do intrude upon attention and control the way it is used. Although the consequences of this intrusion and control can be beneficial if the schemas are positive, there are times when even positive schemas can interfere with the attainment of particular goals or experiences. They also may tend to distract us from noticing and using our unconscious resources.

SOMETIMES AN ABSENCE OF SCHEMAS IS BEST

Thus far, we have concentrated on the benefits of using hypnosis to construct positive schemas. It may surprise the reader, therefore, when we suggest that there are times when an absence of bias, even a positive one, may be best. There are situations in which we need to be able to detach awareness from schematic influences altogether and rely instead on our natural talents and inclinations (cf. Erickson, Rossi, & Rossi, 1976).

Sports and other activities involving coordinated physical movement and situations requiring acts of "spontaneous" mental creativity and insight are good examples of activities that are best performed without schemas. To achieve success in these endeavors, it is best to rely on overlearned or innate skills. Peak physical performance results when our conscious awareness is no longer dominated by the biases and concerns of our schemas (Gallwey, 1974). Problem solving and creativity also seem to require a detached, nonjudgmental observation of events and a willingness to respond in a natural, unrestricted manner (Vernon, 1970).

Schemas or mental sets, even positive ones, can create problems when the task at hand requires us to recognize and utilize previously unconscious resources. As Nuke discovered in the film *Bull Durham*, it takes more than a belief in one's prowess to pitch a ball with grace, skill, and intelligence. Nuke learned that he needed to breathe through his "third eye" (i.e., use his unconscious abilities) in order to pitch at his highest level. The "helpful" comments and coaching instructions of his conscious mind's schemas produced awkwardness and misjudgment rather than superior performance. Like Sergeant Joe Friday of *Dragnet*, the brain and the body need "just the facts, nothing but the facts" in order to react to a situation with natural grace and insight. They need relatively undistorted and complete data about the situation and objective feedback regarding the effects of different responses to that situation. Comments and suggestions from schemas or mental sets merely distract attention and prevent us from focusing on useful information. Behavior and thinking tend to become stilted or uncoordinated under such circumstances. As Erickson observed, "Confusion results from trying to impose some form of regimentation upon natural processes" (Erickson, Rossi, & Rossi, 1976, p. 243).

The ability to enter unusual or altered states of consciousness is also inhibited by our schemas, be they positive or negative. The state of consciousness produced by the constant chatterings and influences of our schemas *is* our ordinary or usual state of consciousness. Therefore, an altered state of consciousness necessarily involves either an alteration of these schemas or their elimination from awareness. Peak experiences may require only a brief suspension of our biases. Transcendental consciousness or *satori*, on the other hand, seems to involve the total elimination of the effects of most of our schemas, including our biased sense of self (cf. Deikman, 1966).

Just as hypnotic trance can be used to create positive schemas, it also can be used to direct attention away from schemas altogether. Before attention can be directed toward new schemas or away from schemas altogether, however, it first must be captured and stabilized.

ATTENTION IS UNSTABLE

Attention can be as jumpy as a nervous colt, skipping untamed from one thing to another. As long as attention keeps jumping about, it is difficult to capture or redirect in more appropriate ways.

Under ordinary circumstances, the focus of attention shifts rapidly from one thing to another in a constant scanning of internal and external events. Moving attention from place to place is an effective way to maintain our conscious orientation in time and space, to respond to threats or emergencies, and to adjust our behavior as events change around us. It enables us to notice discrepancies and keep track of events that might have personal importance to us or our schemas. It allows us to compare all events and behaviors with our beliefs or attitudes about the way things "should" be, and it enables us to adjust our behavior to the changing pattern of events. Above all, it keeps us informed. As Bornstein and Ruddy (1984) note, the more things 4-month-old infants are encouraged to notice in their environment, the higher their intelligence test scores will be at 1 year of age and the greater their vocabularies. When attention moves about, we notice more things and we know more about things.

This instability of attention probably has its roots in our evolutionary history. Nervous scanning of the environment may have been especially useful for our biological ancestors who faced frequent danger and unpredictability. It may well be that the instability of attention was so important that it became one of the basic "defaults" (i.e., sets of rules evolution has programmed into the mind that we follow unless given different instructions) discussed by Ornstein and Ehrlich (1989, p. 91). But this scanning function is far less useful in contemporary situations, especially when it becomes excessive.

Excessive and uncontrollable scanning is partially a reflection of the nervous system's evolutionary-based efforts to construct and maintain a perceptual gestalt of the world, partially a response to the recent rise in environmental "news of differences" or distractions and partially a result of continuous attempts by our mental sets to keep track of and influence all of our conscious perceptions and responses. Excessive scanning often reflects a driven attempt to monitor, and hence control, all present events and all possible future calamities. It is the hallmark of anxiety and fear of failure. Such a strategy allows the individual to skip rapidly from one potential danger to another, but it does not provide for a focused, well-considered response to any one of them.

When, for whatever reason, we scan everything excessively, we obtain little more than fleeting glimpses of events in the internal and external worlds. Like a frantic television viewer "channel surfing" with a remote control, we rarely experience anything in depth and miss much of the action on every channel. We skim the surface of each subject, gleaning only enough to reassure ourselves that everything is in its place and operating as expected. We light on a particular channel only if its content is engaging or promises news of personal interest, but we may not be able to stay tuned in long enough to get the point. Attention moves on, constantly propelled by a concern that we will miss something someplace else.

Even individuals who do not scan excessively find that there are times when it is best to hold the attention still and to become absorbed in one thing—whether it is to learn something new, to relax, to react more effectively, or to free themselves from the constraints of their usual schemas and world view. It is difficult to do so, but not impossible, and the results can be quite beneficial.

THE BENEFITS OF STABLE ATTENTION

Mihaly Csikszentmihalyi, a professor of psychology at the University of Chicago, has spent a large part of his career studying the basis of happiness and enjoyment in life. His careful search for the specific causes of happiness led him to the conclusion that it is based on "a state of concentration so focused that it amounts to absolute absorption in an activity"(Csikszentmihalyi, 1990, frontispiece). Csikszentmihalyi called this ongoing state of selectively focused, undistracted attention "flow." Happy, contented people are those who experience flow, those who are able to manage their attention well enough to become completely absorbed in the activities of the moment.

We often hear reports of this absorption experience from artists and athletes. Race-car drivers, for example, rave about the state of absorption they experience during a race and call it "streaming," while artists frequently note that they worked for hours on a painting without stopping because they became lost in the act of creation. Religious personalities have written of being "transfixed" and scientists report becoming absorbed for weeks or years in a particular problem. All of these are examples of "flow."

Herbert Benson, associate professor of medicine at the Harvard Medical School, also described the benefits of stable attention in his study of intense but short-term experiences of focused attention (Benson, 1975). Benson used a simplified version of a form of meditation to stabilize attention. He asked his subjects to spend 20 minutes twice a day focusing their attention exclusively on the silent mental repetition of the word "one." They would consistently redirect their attention back to the target word whenever their attention wandered, ignoring everything else that might drift into their attention, including their own mental critiques of their performance. After practicing this attention-centering exercise for several weeks, subjects reported that they felt happier, more relaxed, and more competent, both physically and mentally. Benson coined the term "the relaxation response" to describe the highly relaxed, profoundly comfortable state of mind and body that occurs during such periods of intensely focused attention.

Whatever we call these conditions of absorbed concentration, they appear to enhance pleasure and contentment. Absorbed, stabilized attention also seems to be necessary for peak performance. As William James observed in 1890, "But, whether the attention comes by grace of genius or by dint of will, the longer one does attend to a topic, the more mastery of it one has" (Goleman & Davidson, 1979, p. 45). Gallwey (1974) cleverly illustrated the importance of focused attention by pointing out to his tennis students that you cannot hit a ball if you do not see it, and you cannot see it if your mind is wandering in a distracted manner from one thing to another. Competence, health, and happiness all seem to depend on the ability to focus attention.

ON MASTERING ATTENTION

A stable focus of attention is a basic component of wellness, tranquillity, and peak performance. A collection of healthy schemas, such as those that promote optimism, altruism, and interpersonal connectedness, is another. But two roadblocks stand in the way of achieving these pleasant outcomes. The first is the almost inherent instability of attention. The second is the influence on attention of irrelevant, wrong, or counterproductive schemas.

As long as attention wanders about aimlessly or is controlled by unhealthy schemas, our ability to intentionally direct attention toward what we choose, toward information that is useful, and toward thoughts that are comforting is impaired. People who cannot control the stability or contents of their own attention cannot control their own understandings, emotions, or responses.

Although there now is a considerable body of scientific evidence that indicates that attention controls our experience and behavior, this information is used primarily to design cereal boxes, presidential candidates, and beer commercials. These carefully packaged products do engage attention and control behavior, but this fact simply emphasizes the urgency of the need for each individual to learn how to focus attention and take charge of its contents.

To become responsible for our own well-being, we must learn how to focus attention where and how we want and need it to be, not where the advertising agencies or our own critical, pessimistic schemas force it to be. Each individual must learn how to break free of these distracting, destructive influences and to turn his or her attention toward a resolute immersion in self-enhancing attitudes and activities. Our experience suggests that hypnotic trance is a viable and efficient means to these ends. As the material presented in the following chapter indicates, we believe that the Ericksonian approach to hypnosis and hypnotherapy, in particular, provides the tools needed to captivate attention and to stimulate new modes of awareness.

SUMMARY

Attention determines what we experience, what we think about those experiences, and what we do in response to them. Ordinarily, attention is flighty and is dominated by the biases and prejudiced beliefs of our schemas. This may result in unpleasant thoughts and actions, a limited view of reality, and an unintended abandonment of unconscious resources and abilities. To produce the conditions responsible for well-being, we must stabilize attention and either alter the content of schemas in a positive direction or eliminate the effects of such schemas on attention altogether.

3

USING HYPNOSIS

Therapeutic trance is focused attention . . .
(Milton H. Erickson
in Erickson & Rossi, 1979, p. 30)

In the first chapter, we discussed the implications of expanding the practice of hypnotherapy to include the concepts and goals associated with wellness, tranquillity, and peak performance. The roles of attention and schemas in conscious and unconscious functioning were reviewed in Chapter 2. The present chapter examines the relationship between attention and hypnosis. It also explains how to stabilize attention hypnotically and redirect it in ways that produce desired alterations in experience, attitudes, and response.

The information and recommendations presented in this chapter are designed largely for those who consider themselves novices in the field of Ericksonian hypnotherapy. Nonetheless, we hope that those already familiar with the Ericksonian approach will also find something of interest and value here.

THE RELATIONSHIP BETWEEN TRANCE
AND ATTENTION

Two events are characteristic of a trance state. First, attention is focused in a single direction toward a single topic. Because attention ordinarily is so active and involved in scanning the internal and external environment, this period of absorption need only be 15 or 20 seconds to qualify it as a "trance." Second, during trance attention is shifted away from the schemas that ordinarily bias and direct it. The focused absorption of trance frees us momentarily from the critical and analytical guidance of our habitual mental sets.

Whenever attention is captivated by a particular thought, sensation, or perception, we enter the focused absorption characteristic of a trance. Such interludes in ordinary conscious functioning happen to everyone throughout the day. Sometimes we notice them, sometimes we do not. Colloquial terms for this brief type of trance include "spacing out" and "going on automatic pilot." For a moment or two, we are oblivious to the rest of the world and no longer are keeping track of who we are, where we are, or what is going on outside us. Whenever something reminds us of a personal memory or issue, we may begin thinking intently about this topic and become absorbed in our inner experiences. This absorption is trance.

Thus trance occurs naturally in our daily lives. It is an ordinary part of our experience. It is easy to see, then, that hypnotic trance is simply the intentional creation and extension of this normal but haphazardly occurring phenomenon. In contrast to these everyday "trances," when people are hypnotized, their attention is absorbed and focused for long periods, perhaps as long as an hour. During this time, hypnotized subjects observe whatever enters their focus of attention with a detached alertness. A hypnotized person may be surprised or puzzled by what occurs, but will allow it to continue. While in a hypnotic trance, people do not feel inclined to make the effort it takes to censor their perceptions or to bring their responses in line with their usual biases. During hypnosis, painfully shy people are able to visualize a social interaction in which they are relaxed and confident. Writers can enjoy a creativity free from self-conscious concerns. Extroverts experience a calm, internal peace that is contrary to their usual need for continuous external stimulation. Hypnosis liberates us from the biases and controls typically imposed by our schemas.

Although it is something of an oversimplification to suggest that alterations in attention are the basis for hypnotic responses, this conceptualization is quite consistent with the relevant clinical literature and research. It has been clear for many years that hypnosis involves focused attention. In 1845, for example, Charles Radclyffe Hall described trance as a "riveting" of attention and spoke of the "rapt contemplation" and "concentration of the mind" that are crucial to hypnosis (Hall, 1965, pp. 42–52). Experts on the topic of hypnosis, though disagreeing on other theoretical constructs, all seem to concur with Hall that focused attention is a basic ingredient of the development of hypnotic phenomena (e.g., Barber, 1960; Gill & Brenman, 1961; Hull, 1933; Weitzenhoffer, 1953). Pekala and Kumar (1988), using the Phenomenology of Consciousness Inventory, a scale developed by Pekala (1982), investigated the role of attention during hypnosis. As expected, they found that during hypnotic trance attention becomes more absorbed, focused, and internally oriented. They also discovered that, at the same time, hypnotized subjects feel less of a need to remain vigilant and tend to relinquish efforts to control or censor attention.

Milton Erickson was quite straightforward in describing the alterations of attention characteristic of hypnotic trance. For example, he once observed, "All hypnosis is, is a loss of the multiplicity of the foci of attention. . . . It is a lack of response to irrelevant external stimuli (Erickson & Rossi, 1981, pp. 187–188). Erickson's students also have emphasized the role of fixed attention in their descriptions of hypnosis (e.g., Gilligan, 1987; Lankton & Lankton, 1986, 1989; Zeig, 1988).

Defining hypnosis as a process of capturing and redirecting attention not only is consistent with clinical and scientific observations, but it has other advantages as well. First, a focus on attention demystifies the hypnotic process. We intentionally define hypnosis as something that is rather ordinary and easy to understand, that is, as focused attention. This view of hypnosis does not require the reader to adopt a new theoretical orientation or develop a new vocabulary.

Second, and more important, if hypnotic trance is viewed as a means of redirecting attention in a "bias-free" atmosphere, then "trance training" offers people the possibility of adopting entirely new patterns of attention and response. They can use the trance state to "pay attention" to the thoughts and perceptions that lead to wellness, tranquillity, and peak performance. Pessimistic, self-critical schemas may be replaced with more optimistic, self-affirming sets or categories. Hostile reactions, which are hard on the heart, may be tempered with tolerance. People can be encouraged to focus on the humorous and pleasurable events of life, thereby enhancing feelings of well-being and improving health as well.

Erickson once stated, "If I were having my chauffeur drive me in dangerous traffic, I would put him in a deep trance. I would want him to pay attention to the traffic problem. . . . I wouldn't want anything outside the car to distract him . . ." (Zeig, 1980, pp. 227–228). This suggests that there is an optimal attentional set for any activity and that trance can be used to create that optimal condition. We believe this to be the case. There is an optimal state of attention for running marathons, for solving problems, for accepting changes and challenges, and for experiencing cosmic consciousness. According to Walters (1988b), there even is an optimal state of attention for the adoption of a feminist perspective, a state of attention similar to the hypnotic trance. Each of these "trances" involves the refocusing of attention toward those inner and outer events that create the climate necessary for the accomplishment of a particular activity or state of mind.

Hypnotic trance distills attention into a purer form that is at once more malleable and more stable. Once in that form, attention can be molded to maximize the particular thoughts and attitudes that are compatible with the client's goals. Thus hypnotic trance can be used to establish new schemas; it allows us to "set" our minds in whatever directions we choose. By learning how to use hypnosis with your clients, you learn how to make new kinds of thinking and new ways of handling situations available to your clients. You give them the tools needed for personal liberation, optimal functioning, and expanded well-being.

TRADITIONAL AND ERICKSONIAN
HYPNOTIC TECHNIQUES

When we ask our new clients what they know about hypnosis, they generally describe scenes from movies or television. In these scenes, the hypnotist may swing a watch or other object in front of the subject's face or ask the subject to stare at a candle or a picture on the wall. As the subject does so, the hypnotist repeats such directives as, "You are becoming more and more tired, more and more tired. You are becoming tired and sleepy, tired and sleepy. Your eyes are heavy, heavier and heavier. You are getting sleepy, sleepy, sleepy, and you will go into a deep, deep trance. . . ." This approach is the one most people think of as hypnosis, and it is, if one removes the dramatics, quite close to traditional hypnotic techniques. Both rely on the use of emphatic directives telling the subject to focus attention on something and go into a trance. The primary difference between the enactments of hypnosis on television and a real trance session is that on television the subjects always go into a trance, whereas in real life they often do not.

Does this mean that there are many people who cannot be hypnotized? Not necessarily. It does mean that many people respond poorly to a directive style of hypnosis. In fact, Pekala and Kumar (1988) observed that directive hypnotic procedures upset or confuse people, often leaving them even less focused than they were prior to the induction. Hilgard (1965) found that only 12 percent to 18 percent of the population are able to enter a trance or experience hypnotic phenomena when a directive approach is used. Only people who already know how to focus their attention in an absorbed manner (i.e., those who already tend to get lost in their own thoughts) respond well to such directives. Hilgard called the ability to get lost in one's own thoughts "imaginative involvement."

Erickson understood the relevance of imaginative involvement to hypnosis. He also recognized that most people are not skilled at imaginative involvement and have to be taught how to focus attention in this absorbed manner. Therefore, he created hypnotic induction techniques that, in themselves, initiate a trance state. Because attention is captured by things that are new, unexpected, or unusual (cf. Broadbent, 1958), Erickson relied on the new, the unusual, and the unexpected to induce a trance. He used shock, surprise, ambiguity, contradictions, and even boredom to redirect a subject's attention away from conscious distractions and toward an internal focus (cf. Erickson, Rossi, & Rossi, 1976).

Erickson was a skilled communicator. He used his facility with communication to grab people's attention and lead them into a trance. The attention-grabbing techniques Erickson used bear a striking resemblance to those recommended in the literature on classical rhetoric.

Rhetoric is the art of persuasive communication. The skilled rhetorician uses puns, word plays, truisms, metaphors, and anecdotes to capture attention and put the audience in a receptive frame of mind (Dixon, 1971). Erickson certainly was a master of these rhetorical skills. He knew how to get people's attention! The Ericksonian procedures do develop absorbed attention. Havens (1991) utilized these techniques to induce trance. Subjects subsequently reported significant increases in their experiences of absorbed attention.

Once attention is captured, the stage is set for a therapeutic use of hypnosis. Like rhetoric, the goal of hypnotherapy is to alter basic points of view (schemas) and change behavior. Like a rhetorician, the hypnotherapist must communicate in a way that influences thoughts and actions while deflecting critical analysis. Erickson, along with most orators, relied on metaphors and metaphorical anecdotes to direct captivated attention toward new ideas.

COMMUNICATING WITH METAPHORS
AND ANECDOTES

Metaphor is a word, phrase, or entire story that is used to imply a likeness or analogy between one object or idea and another. For example, terms that originally applied only to living beings often are used metaphorically when discussing inanimate objects and everyday events. We talk about rust "eating" a car "body" as if that were an accurate description of the processes and materials involved. Similarly, the computer–brain metaphor is so compelling that we now talk about "programming" the brain and the "memory" of a computer as if these two objects were in fact identical in structure and operation. Obviously they are not, but the use of metaphorical references makes it seem as if they are. Metaphors use what we know about one thing to bridge gaps in our understanding about something else. They transfer meaning from one place to another by implying that our thoughts or feelings about one situation are relevant to the other. They suggest and create a linkage.

Many therapists recognize the value of metaphors in clinical work, and metaphorical anecdotes are consistently emphasized in discussions of Ericksonian approaches to hypnosis and hypnotherapy. Zeig (1980), for example, presents an extensive analysis of Erickson's use of metaphorical anecdotes. He lists their many advantages (e.g., they are nonthreatening, engaging, memorable) and describes their hypnotherapeutic applications (e.g., to illustrate a point, to suggest solutions, to increase motivation, to embed directives). Similarly, Lankton and Lankton (1983) discuss the structure and purposes of the various types of metaphors used by Erickson and describe how to use several different metaphors at a time to avoid conscious resistance to the underlying implications. Gilligan (1987) explored the importance of metaphorical processing in hypnosis, referring to it as "a central and unifying concept of the Ericksonian approach" (p. 56). Rosen (1982) apparently viewed Erickson's metaphorical anecdotes as so central to the Ericksonian therapeutic process that he published a collection of over 100 of them. Many others (e.g., Barker, 1985; Dolan, 1986; Fantz, 1983; Gordon, 1978; Matthews & Dardeck, 1985; Mills & Crowley, 1986; O'Hanlon, 1986; Welch, 1984) have published professional books and journal articles devoted almost exclusively to an analysis of the uses of metaphors in therapy.

This emphasis on metaphors in the therapy literature indicates that they must be important. What is it about metaphors that makes them so central both to rhetoric and to the hypnotherapeutic process? To answer this question, we must examine metaphor as a concept.

Theorists of the "constructivist camp" (cf. Ortony, 1979), maintain that the metaphor is the foundation of thought and language. Constructivists suggest that most words in our language, and hence most thoughts as well, began as metaphors. This should not surprise us. After all, it is much easier to borrow old terms that appear to have some relevance than to make up a new term for every new object, situation, or idea. By using the word "wing" when referring to a part of an airplane, we simplify the language and convey something about the function of that part of the plane at the same time. Our reliance on metaphors also reflects our tendency to think in pictures and stories that impose maps of our previous experiences on current situations. Almost everything we learn we grasp by relating it to something we already know. Indeed, some would argue that we are "wired" to think and speak in this fashion, busily transferring ideas from one context to another (cf. Bateson, 1972, 1979).

Most of our language and many of our cognitions are constructed out of metaphors. Consider, for example, the way we speak about the operations of our government. We have a "head" of state, legislative "bodies," and the "arms" or "branches" that carry out the "decisions" of the "head." The armed services are the "muscle," the CIA is our country's "eyes and ears," and the bureaucracy is a "nerve center." Such terms are so embedded in our *lingua franca* that we seldom recognize their metaphorical origins. Even scientific constructs and theories are metaphorical. The wave/particle metaphors physicists use today to describe the structure of the universe may seem to be more sophisticated than the religious metaphors used during the Middle Ages, but they are metaphors nonetheless, attempts to use the motion of billiard balls and waves in water to describe what happens at another level of reality. Psychologists have borrowed concepts from various fields, such as hydraulics, acting, and computer science, to explain human behavior. The metaphorical basis of psychological theories is reviewed in a collection of essays edited by Leary (1990).

In addition to forming much of the structural basis for thought and language, metaphors also are the foundation for *new* understandings, perspectives, and ideas. According to some constructivists (e.g., MacCormac, 1985), new ideas are born from the use of new metaphors to describe something old and familiar or the use of old metaphors to describe something new and unfamiliar— new wine in old skins or old wine in new skins, to apply a biblical metaphor to the issue. At first, old terms about the brain were used to describe the operation of computers. Computers were given "memories" and "languages." Now we have begun to use computer terms and concepts to revise our thinking about the operation of the brain. "Parallel processing," "neurolinguistic programming," and "neural circuitry" are some examples. Our entire way of thinking about the operations of the brain versus the computer has come full circle. Where we once defined computers in terms of their similarities to the brain, we now talk about the brain in terms that make it sound similar to a computer. Our understanding of how brains and computers operate changes depending on the metaphor applied.

In the same manner, our self-perception depends on the metaphors we use to describe ourselves. If we imagine ourselves to be important cogs or gears in the machinery of civilization, it is obvious that we must work hard to keep up our function and to produce the desired products. On the other hand, if we view ourselves as slaves of the system, we may acquire more rebellious attitudes. Similarly, an individual who views each new situation metaphorically as a dangerous gamble will respond differently from the person who applies a metaphor of exploration, discovery, and opportunity to each of life's twists and turns. One will hesitate to turn a new corner and the other will be drawn forward by curiosity and anticipation of unseen treasure. As this suggests, the metaphors we adopt about ourselves and the world influence our schemas, and our schemas, in turn, influence the metaphors we choose.

This answers our previous question as to why scholars of rhetoric, as well as many therapists, emphasize metaphors in their work. Metaphors are useful devices for directing attention toward new ideas or principles. Metaphors capture attention and provide new or different ways of looking at things. Metaphors can play a dominant role in the redirection of awareness toward concepts the presenter wishes the audience to examine and apply in a new way to produce new schemas.

A simple metaphor, such as "the mask of sanity," captures the imagination. For a moment, our view of "reality" may shift. Old elements of our schemas are replaced by new ones. Unmasking hidden metaphors can have a similar effect. Consider, for example, the impact on our feelings about our careers as professional therapists when we recognize that the word "career" is an ancient sailing term used to describe a vessel on a course that takes it full speed ahead, or that the term "professional" originally referred to a person who had professed an acceptance of the rules and beliefs of a religious order and been accepted into that religious community. Metaphors make us stop and consider as we integrate one idea with another.

All cultures have their "teaching tales," that is, the myths and stories used to edify and instruct. Fairy tales, such as *The Ugly Duckling*, offer metaphorical messages, as do biblical parables, Greek myths, and Zen koans. In fact, Zen koans (e.g., "Zen is a finger pointing at the moon") are often sophisticated metaphors developed to create trance-inducing challenges to existing perspectives (cf. Ornstein, 1986). To comprehend their meaning, the pupil must ignore the interpretations or reactions of existing schemas and allow his or her most literal unconscious schemas to enter awareness. They require and reveal a completely new way of thinking, a new set of assumptions and concepts.

If we wish to hold attention for a long time and suggest a broad set of relationships, we can use a metaphorical anecdote. A good storyteller can hold an audience spellbound. The success of humorist Garrison Keilor and his mythical stories of Lake Wobegon bear witness to this. If a story is entertaining, people will pay attention to it. If it offers metaphorical references relevant to the attitudes and actions of the audience, it may trigger significant changes in their feelings and behavior. Often the audience will identify with the main character and incorporate his or her qualities and responses into their schemas about themselves. *The Ugly Duckling*, for example, is designed to provide children with the reassuring idea that eventually they will transcend their present discomforts and find a place where they belong.

A scene in the movie *What About Bob?* also demonstrates the power of metaphors quite nicely. In a desperate effort to rid himself once and for all of Bob, an intrusive and demanding patient, Bob's therapist takes him into the woods, ties him up, and places a satchel of explosives on his lap with a timer set to go off in several minutes. As Bob struggles to free himself, he naïvely muses about the message his therapist is trying to convey with this "exercise." He eventually decides that his therapist is trying to tell him that he is all tied up in knots inside, and that unless he frees himself from these binding restrictions, he will explode emotionally and psychologically. Having deciphered the metaphorical implications of the situation, Bob escapes his bonds and goes off to tell his therapist about the profound change in perspective this experience has created. (We do not recommend this particular exercise, but metaphorical exercises can be just as effective therapeutically as metaphorical anecdotes.)

Attention is fixed during hypnosis. As attention stabilizes and the mind's schema-based comments drift into the background of awareness, people are able to listen more carefully and to absorb new thoughts, ideas, and experiences more completely. Metaphors can convey their messages more easily during trance because the individual is listening in a more open, less critical manner. But metaphors and metaphorical anecdotes are also effective without a hypnotic trance because they present their therapeutic concepts indirectly and are themselves somewhat trance inducing.

Whether used with or without a hypnotic trance, the metaphorical approach captures attention. It also neutralizes the common tendency to resist change because the metaphor requires listeners to construct whatever mental bridges exist between the story and its logical applications to themselves (as Bob did). The listeners are responsible for grasping the analogy in the form they choose; they are responsible for mentally constructing relationships between what is being presented and possible implications for their own schemas and behaviors. If a therapist tells a story about the hunting methods of an African tribe or a 19th-century quilting circle, it is up to the listeners, the clients, to determine what the events in this story have to do with them. They do not know whether they should identify with the people in the story, learn from their example, or merely enjoy a good tale. Nothing is forced on the listeners; they are free to come to their own conclusions. Hence there is nothing to resist.

The relatively ambiguous quality of many metaphors contributes to the process of individualized interpretation and understanding. Sometimes clients replace the message you intend to convey with a different, often more useful, interpretation. Indeed, we hope our clients will do just that. Such fortuitous events expand the potential value of metaphorical communications in a therapeutic setting. Each person can discover his or her own unique set of implications and relationships in the stories provided by the therapist and apply them in a unique manner to his or her life and needs.

Hypnosis amplifies the captivating and stimulating qualities of metaphors, but it does not create them. Metaphorical anecdotes intrigue us, capture our attention, and direct our thoughts toward particular topics. The metaphors incorporated into our scripts were selected because they interest people and hold their attention. Each describes attitudes, experiences, and conceptual orientations consistent with the pursuit of a richer, more fulfilling life. We may intend them to alter attentional biases in specific ways, but we recognize that they will convey different messages to each listener. Because we believe that each individual is inherently self-correcting and self-healing when loosened from the restrictions of his or her rigid schemas or mental sets, we assume that each person will decipher a meaning from our metaphors that is most relevant and useful at the time. We depend on it. Metaphors offer alternative ways of thinking and doing; they point the person in new directions. But each individual expands awareness and understanding in whatever way is most appropriate for him or her. The recommendations contained in metaphors are a bit like Joseph Campbell's advice, "Follow your bliss." They point in the general direction, but they leave the specifics up to the individual.

STEPS IN THE HYPNOTIC PROCESS

The purpose of a hypnotic intervention is to capture attention, direct it away from existing schemas, and focus it on the therapeutic message of the hypnotist or the responses of the unconscious mind. There are many different ways to accomplish this purpose.

One hypnotist might use a brief informal approach, embedding the hypnotic process in a seemingly unrelated conversation about a topic of interest to the client, such as tomato plants. Erickson did exactly that with a man who was suffering the severe chronic pain of cancer (Erickson, 1966). By emphasizing certain key words and phrases, Erickson captured the patient's attention and directed it toward thoughts and feelings associated with comfort. He used this indirect, conversational approach because the man needed and wanted his help but his schemas did not allow him to believe in hypnosis. Erickson bypassed this resistance by using a conversational style of hypnosis to present a metaphorical discussion of comfort that was inherently captivating and trance inducing.

A different hypnotist, or Erickson on a different occasion, might conduct a more formalized hypnosis session, using some of the rituals traditionally associated with hypnosis. For example, one subject might be told to stare at an object embedded in a glass paperweight until his or her eyes become so tired and heavy that they close by themselves. Another might be asked to observe the changes in sensation in a hand or arm as that arm gets lighter and begins to move up by itself. In a less formalized approach, the subject might simply be asked to close his or her eyes and to listen to the things the hypnotist says. This is the approach we prefer and use in a majority of the sessions recorded in the scripts in Part II of this text.

No matter what style the hypnotist employs, however, the overall purpose is the same in each instance, that is, to focus attention on certain ideas and responses. Accordingly, a majority of hypnosis sessions follow these same basic steps.

1. *A transition from an ordinary conversation into a hypnotic process.* This is accomplished most easily by straightforwardly asking your client if it is acceptable to use hypnosis at that point. If your subject agrees, you may ask him or her to move to a more comfortable chair and close his or her eyes, or just have the client close his or her eyes where he or she is sitting. It is not absolutely necessary to inform a client that you plan to use a trance-inducing procedure or to ask permission to do so, but we highly recommend it. It sets the hypnosis session apart as something special, maintains trust and rapport, and initiates cooperation.

2. *A trance induction to capture and calm attention and redirect it away from existing schemas or mental sets.* The trance induction is a series of statements that capture attention and reassure the participant, preparing him or her for an inner journey into new realms of experience. The induction provides an opportunity to quiet the "chattering monkey" that continually distracts attention. As attention settles down and becomes absorbed by things other than the worries and comments of the ordinary schemas, spontaneous alterations in inner and outer reality become easier to notice and accept. The trance induction scripts in this book demonstrate various approaches for accomplishing this goal in a comfortable and creative fashion.

3. *Metaphorical guidance and/or direct suggestions that stimulate unconscious understandings and responses.* As trance develops, people become open to new ideas, new challenges, and new perspectives. Metaphors guide the mind down new paths toward new schemas and new self-identities. Sometimes metaphors are used to identify and erode biases that block further growth. Sometimes they simply direct attention toward comfortable ways of being and provide the permission needed to adopt these roles in everyday life. Some stories remind the listener of soothing memories and some encourage self-care. Others may describe an exuberant lack of self-consciousness in the performance of some activity. We select and shape metaphors to fit the interests, experiences, and goals of the participant, but we also assume that participants will shape their interpretations and responses to fit their own needs.

   There are times when a direct, nonmetaphorical presentation of ideas may be used to channel learning in new directions or toward unconscious connections to the ingredients of well-being. Similarly, direct suggestions can be used as a straightforward way to elicit unconscious responses in some instances. These direct approaches are an efficient way to accomplish the desired outcomes, but they are useful primarily with subjects who are in a deep trance or who are completely disconnected from the instructions and controls imposed by a concerned and resistant set of conscious schemas.

4. *An opportunity for the participant to rehearse or practice new skills and attitudes.* Because responsibility for future growth and change lies within each individual, we encourage participants to reinstate intentionally the focused attention of trance and to rehearse the specific alterations in attention that were dealt with during the trance session. This enables the subject to master his or her own attentional processes and to take charge of the attitudes, behaviors, and experi-

ences central to each session. It allows new schemas to become organized into coherent sets of attitudes or responses and firmly implanted in the mind. Examples of this process are incorporated into several of the hypnotherapeutic scripts in Part II.

5. *Ending a trance session.* Hypnosis is an interactive, cooperative endeavor. The therapist seeks to create a climate conducive to trance experiences. Ultimately, however, it is up to the client to choose how and when to participate. The hypnotic subject can choose whether to allow attention to become focused and whether to become absorbed by new knowledge and experiences. Even when the hypnotist is able to create a safe, supportive environment, each individual will participate in whatever way is appropriate and comfortable at the time.

   Accordingly, it also is up to each individual to reestablish a normal, wakeful focus of attention. The hypnotist helps redirect attention back to the sounds in the room and to a wakeful pattern of experience, but it is the client who actually does the reorienting. Some clients will take longer than others to do so, and some may choose to remain in a trance for an extended period. Remember, people do not become automatons during hypnosis. Thus they do not get "stuck" in a trance. Even if you were to leave the room without mentioning that they should wake up, they would do so eventually on their own.

   Each of our hypnotherapy scripts ends with a slightly different trance termination procedure to demonstrate different styles of communicating that it is time to quit. There is no magic formula to it any more than there is a magic formula to the rest of the trance process. Usually, a simple comment, such as, "OK, it is time to wake up now," is sufficient.

6. *Ratifying the trance.* Many of our hypnosis scripts incorporate a trance ratification experience into the trance termination procedure. A trance ratification experience is any

event that convinces the hypnotic subject that he or she just underwent something very different from, and in some ways more powerful than, ordinary waking consciousness. It validates the reality of the trance and the reality of the unconscious abilities that the trance released. Just in case the hypnotic process itself did not contain such an experience, we sometimes end with a suggestion designed to elicit a pleasant but surprising or puzzling event as the subject returns to a waking state. Brief periods of immobility, heightened sensations of warmth or coolness, and partial amnesia all are examples of possible trance ratification experiences.

The steps listed represent a general outline for hypnosis sessions. In actual practice, these steps do not occur as discrete or separate events. Rather, they tend to blend together in an ongoing flow. For example, trance induction comments are usually interspersed throughout the session, amplifying and deepening the trance. Metaphors may be included in the initial induction process. In fact, a session may begin with a long metaphorical anecdote to capture attention and describe the trance desired.

There are no absolutes, no set rituals to be used on all occasions with all subjects. The hypnotherapist is guided by therapeutic goals, by an understanding of the trance experience, and by the unique interests and needs of a specific client. Like an abstract expressionist artist, the hypnotist decides how to use a palette of colorful words to fill a waiting canvas. The finished product will contain shapes, rhythms, and symbols that capture attention and evoke a different response in each viewer. We can offer general "criteria" and a paint-by-numbers canvas in the form of scripts. You can use the scripts to practice, but eventually you will want to strike off on your own.

LEARNING TO MANAGE ATTENTION
WITH "HYPNOSIS"

Many professionals are reluctant to use hypnosis in their practices even after they have been through several training sessions or workshops. No matter how many lectures they attend or books they read, they remain uncomfortable about adding hypnosis to their repertoire of therapeutic skills.

Some of this reluctance may be the result of the mystico-religious connotations the term "hypnosis" has taken on in our culture. Many religious groups still label it the work of the devil, and there are professionals who argue that hypnosis is nothing more than pure hokum. Books about hypnosis published for the popular market have done little to improve the situation. They make fantastic claims about the power of hypnosis and present it as a gateway into extrasensory abilities or past lives. It is not surprising that both professionals and lay-persons remain skeptical about hypnosis.

Perhaps it is time to select a new term to describe the procedures and phenomena we call "hypnosis." "Attention management," for example, offers a more accurate description of the process and does not have hundreds of years of myths and misconceptions attached to it. Professionals might find teaching the skills of attention management a more palatable assignment, and the public might be more receptive to learning something called attention management.

Realizing that old traditions die hard, however, we will, at least for the moment, continue to use the term hypnosis. Accordingly, here are some suggestions to foster the development of your hypnotic abilities.

1. Mastering the hypnotic process involves experiencing it yourself. Once you have experienced the trance state, it no longer seems like strange or unfamiliar territory. It is easier

to facilitate an experience in others when you are comfortable and familiar with that experience yourself.

If possible, work with a colleague who is familiar with hypnotic procedures and willing to help you experience the trance state. If this is not possible, you may wish to record and use one of the sample induction scripts provided later. Or you may order a tape, *An Orientation to the Trance Experience*, we produced especially for this purpose (Havens & Walters, 1989a).

2. Seek out supervision and training from experienced practitioners, qualified workshop leaders, or professional hypnosis organizations. As with any skill, a basic ability to utilize hypnotic procedures can be acquired by reading and practicing, but the advice and feedback of experts help to develop those skills.

3. To practice your trance delivery, pick one of our induction scripts and read it out loud. Record it if you can, and then listen to the tone and rhythm of your presentation. Notice if it is too fast or too loud. Put yourself in the shoes of the listener. Does it capture your attention and move you toward a trance state, or does it sound awkward and jarring at times? A smooth and soothing style is most conducive to the development of a trance.

The format of the scripts presented throughout Part II is designed to convey the rhythm, phrasing, and emphasis appropriate for hypnosis. Each word is best presented slowly with a pause between each line of text. Use a longer pause between sentences. Words in **bold** type need added emphasis, whereas words in *italics* need to be spoken more softly. These changes in rhythm and emphasis give the listener time to comprehend the multiple meanings and to develop and observe his or her own trance responses. A rhythmic, compelling trance delivery also will be facilitated by entering a hypnotic trance state yourself.

4. Study the way puns, rhymes, plays on words, metaphorical

anecdotes, and other verbal devices are incorporated into the trance process in our scripts. There often is a poetic quality to the rhythms and rhymes in these scripts. This is intentional. An engaging presentation captivates attention and depotentiates the conscious resistance inherent in any individual's schemas. The listener floats along with the words, allowing them to create images, tap memories, and evoke experiences. This is the essence of an indirect approach to hypnotic communications.

5. Notice also the way in which direct suggestions are embedded in the patter at times and are offered very straightforwardly at others. We tend to use a rather straightforward approach when attempting to elicit specific alterations in sensory experiences and an indirect, metaphorical approach when dealing with alterations in schematic biases. Even when the request for a response is fairly direct, however, we never demand or require it. Demands for compliance or orders for a specific experience are inappropriate challenges of the client's freedom. Not only are they rarely successful, but they interfere with the cooperative mutuality of the trance process.

PRETRANCE PREPARATIONS

Before you begin to use trance with any individual or group, remember that your purpose is to create an interpersonal and physical climate that will foster focused, schema-free observation or absorption. This climate is highly dependent on your actions and demeanor. Thus it is critical that your behavior and mental sets be compatible with the following principles.

1. *The subject's well-being is the only concern.* Hypnosis is used to enhance the subject's comfort, to develop his or her self-awareness, and to expand his or her abilities. It is not used to increase the hypnotist's prestige or influence. As Mahoney

(1991) suggests, it is useful to prepare for each session by reaffirming the desire to help.

2. *The subject decides what will happen and what will not.* The hypnotist must approach the process with a willingness to give the subject freedom to respond in whatever way is most comfortable. There can be no effort to impose an experience or a response on the subject even if the therapist believes it to be "in the client's best interests."

3. *The subject must be protected at all times.* This includes physical, psychological, and emotional protection. Subjects need to be protected from ridicule, from invasions of privacy, from premature knowledge of traumatic memories, and from all forms of attack or censure.

4. *The personal anxieties of the hypnotist have no place in a session.* Prior to each session, the hypnotist should take a few minutes to relax, enter a calmly centered state, and let go of all personal issues. This will initiate a calm climate for the session and enable the hypnotist to focus her or his full attention on the subject.

5. *A peaceful environment helps the subject and the hypnotist.* Most people find it easier to focus their attention and enter a trance when faced with few distractions. Thus we recommend a quiet environment where the subject can be physically and emotionally comfortable. Seating, lighting, and so on can be arranged with this in mind.

Schemas, even harsh, rigid ones, provide a certain protective guidance. People must feel comfortable and protected if they are to let go of their schemas and enter a state in which they feel free to allow whatever happens to "just happen." This means that your own critical or self-conscious schemas need to stay out of the interaction. Anything the client does is fine. He or she may feel nervous, awkward, or embarrassed. Whatever happens, the hypnotherapist's position is one of nonevaluative support and acceptance.

CONDUCTING A HYPNOSIS SESSION

We suggest that you begin simply, doing basic inductions that teach clients to focus and stabilize their attention. Most subjects find this experience quite pleasant. They are usually eager to discuss their experiences and to provide you with feedback. Find out what made it easier and what, if anything, seemed to interfere with their trance experience.

Your trance inductions will be smoother and more comfortable if you keep the following suggestions in mind.

1. Take a few moments before the start of any trance procedure to monitor the breathing rhythm of the subject. Regulate your speaking with the subject's breathing pattern, speaking as he or she exhales, pausing as he or she inhales. Then gradually slow the pace of your presentation. Usually, the client will respond to this by breathing more slowly and becoming more relaxed. Then slow down even more. It is almost impossible to speak too slowly to someone in a trance, but it is very easy to speak too fast.

2. A trance induction typically begins with a description of what the subject is doing or experiencing at that moment. The subject is sitting in the chair, is breathing in and out, is thinking many different things, is aware of different sensations. By mentioning something you know is happening at that very moment, you capture attention and provide reassurance that you know what is going on and what you are doing. This reassures the client that it is safe to relax and allow attention to drift along with your words.

3. When a subject's attention is restfully focused on your words and on his or her inner responses to those words, you have begun the trance induction. The next step is to present ideas and images that deepen the trance and further stabilize attentional focus. Descriptions of idyllic scenes, captivating

stories, and/or information presented in a poetic style are all useful here.

4. Most clients will reorient at some point during the trance. When clients swallow, shift position a bit, or demonstrate a sudden change in eye movement patterns, they may be experiencing such a reorientation. These reorientations are normal and usually are brief. If this happens, simply reassure the client that everything is fine and lead him or her back into the absorbed attention of trance. A simple, "That's right, and you can drift back into a trance just as easily as you drift upwards," is usually sufficient.

5. Once attention is focused or stabilized and disconnected from the concerns and controls ordinarily imposed by conscious schemas, you are ready to go beyond the induction stage. Gently redirect the client's attention toward ideas, experiences, and understandings that are most compatible with the needs and goals of the client. Use metaphors and anecdotes to stimulate associations and feelings that will lead the client in new directions.

The specific goals and procedures used with any given client depend on the needs and interests of that unique individual. The client's reasons for contacting the hypnotist play a large role in the selection of an appropriate hypnotic procedure, that is, the metaphors employed and the messages they are designed to convey. But the client's reactions to the initial stages of the hypnotic process also help determine what to do next. Although the procedures described in this text are appropriate for most people, some individuals enter into unpleasant thoughts or memories almost as soon as they close their eyes and begin to relax. If such experiences are so distracting and disconcerting that they interfere with the acquisition of positive schemas, the hypnotherapeutic procedures described in our previous book (i.e., Havens & Walters, 1989b) may be needed to quiet or eliminate them. Once this is accomplished, the creation of the ingredients necessary for mental, physical, and emotional well-being remains the fundamental goal.

SUMMARY

Hypnosis stabilizes attention and redirects it toward inner, unconscious responses relevant to the client's goals. Specific forms of speech, including metaphors, appear to facilitate this experience. The hypnotist's optimistic attitude and protective actions also help to establish a climate conducive to the hypnotic experience.

Hypnotic trance can be used to direct attention toward self-affirming attitudes and perceptions and to alter patterns of behavior in healthy directions. Trance experiences also can be used to teach people how to manage the stability and focal content of attention more efficiently.

PART II

Trance Scripts

4

TRANCE INDUCTIONS

This chapter contains a variety of trance induction scripts, each of which demonstrates a slightly different approach to the induction process. All, however, are based on the same conceptualization of the purposes of a trance induction, that is, to stabilize attention and to promote an "observer" role free of interference from the schemas that ordinarily distort awareness and limit responses.

Without assistance, most of us do not have the degree of imaginative involvement necessary to accomplish the trance state. Our minds continue to wander about even while we are trying to pay attention. We modify or critique our experiences in accord with our mental schemas, even when we are trying to be quietly observant.

Thus the initial communications of the hypnotist in our scripts are designed to acknowledge these experiences and the concerns of the subject and to reassure him or her that they are perfectly appropriate. Feelings of uneasiness or confusion are recognized as natural and normal. The rapidly changing contents of attention are described. Over time, attention is gently redirected toward a more stable, observant state of mind. Interesting topics and comments are interspersed with indications that it would be appropriate and safe to allow the "unconscious" mind to assume responsibility for everything for a while. The subject is encouraged just to sit back and watch what happens.

Particular words, phrases, rhythms, rhymes, and other verbal, as well as nonverbal, patterns that tend to capture and soothe attention and to place the person in a receptively observant state of mind are employed throughout each script. In some ways, these trance inductions are similar to many music videos in that they begin with a rapidly changing series of images or thoughts presented in a rhythmic, poetic fashion and offer various symbols and allusions that have multiple meanings. Once attention is captured in this manner, images or thoughts are described in more and more detail and the metaphorical anecdotes become increasingly complex.

As the subject relaxes, ideas are presented more slowly and in more detail. This increases absorption and allows the subject adequate time to grasp both the direct and implicit communications involved. Because each concept or metaphor must be analyzed at many different levels and because each individual word may trigger a wide range of associations, there is no rush. Clients need time to make changes and to have those changes become "set" into permanent alterations in learning and response.

The initial trance process is a good time to teach subjects about their autohypnotic abilities. Autohypnosis is a valuable skill that makes future trance work much simpler. Just experiencing a trance state will accomplish this to some extent, but it also is useful to provide a direct demonstration of the subject's own ability to recreate the trance. One of the scripts presented teaches clients to return to a waking state and then reenter a trance state on their own. Going in and out of trance several times embeds the experience and enables the subject to reestablish the focused and unbiased condition of trance more easily in the future.

Our scripts are designed to serve as guidelines—as exemplary templates that you can use to guide your own creativity. The procedures demonstrated in them are quite generic in character, applicable to almost anyone. Most are so general that they even can be used with some success with large groups. As you become comfortable using hypnosis, you will want to create your own hypnotherapy scripts, individualizing them to meet the unique needs of your clients. Hypnotherapy that is metaphorically or directly relevant to your clients' interests and needs is much more interesting and so is more likely to precipitate alterations in thought and action. Consequently, Chapter 14 offers instructions for writing your own hypnotherapy scripts.

Before you actually attempt a trance induction, the issue of *confident expectancy* must be mentioned. Erickson expected his clients to experience therapeutic change and he instilled the same expectation in them. He also approached the hypnotic situation with a positive expectancy. Sometimes, Erickson simply stared at a hypnotic subject with the confident expectation that the person would enter a trance. This worked for Erickson because he expected it to work; he expected his subjects to enter a trance and they knew he expected them to do so. The trance inductions presented in our scripts also can—and do—work, but their effectiveness can be enhanced (or minimized) by the expectations of the hypnotist. You could probably read a telephone book to many subjects and create a trance state, *if* you expected that outcome. The more confidence you have in the procedures you use, in your subject's ability to respond, in the value of your overall goals, and in yourself, the more positive the outcome will be.

Note: All of the trance procedures presented in later chapters begin with the assumption that the participant has already experienced a successful trance induction.

TRAVELING BEYOND BOUNDARIES

A Basic Trance Induction and Reorientation Script

And so,
as you sit there
in that chair,
with your eyes closed,
you may begin to notice
how things change
as you begin
to rearrange yourself
into a trance,
which at first
may seem quite difficult,
or confusing,
but later on
will become easier
and easier to allow,
though for now
it is enough
just to realize
that you can be aware
of many things there
that otherwise
would have gone overlooked,
or ignored.
You may be more aware
of particular thoughts,
or sensations in an arm,
or a leg,
less aware
of the things around the room,
as you sit there,
feeling the chair
that supports your weight
without needing
to make an effort,
your legs can relax,
no need to hold them there,
your arms can relax
and drift anywhere at all,
just as the mind relaxes
and begins to drift later on,
with the recognition
that there really is no need
to make the effort it takes
to be aware.
You can allow
the body to relax,
the mind to relax,
drifting down
as your breath
drifts out,
and deeper down
as your mind drifts out
and begins to feel
that feeling of safe quietness
and calm letting go,
down deep below,
where there is no need
to pay close attention
to particular things . . . ,
no need to make the effort
to be aware
of taking care,
easier just to allow
the unconscious mind

to take care of things
for **you** for a while.
Because you can relax
in that safe, quiet place,
that deep inner space
where the mind drifts,
almost automatically
as you allow it to do so,
drifting away to other places,
other spaces,
places you may have been,
or only dreamed of going
        before,
away from it all,
a vacation from it all,
perhaps to that balcony
in the Hotel Excelsior,
dining while looking out,
wondering about Florence,
and how it came to be
so beautiful,
with its sidewalk cafes
and lovely art galleries,
or the pink street lights
in St. Mary's Square,
Venice, where you can float
in a boat, a gondola,
under bridges, past mansions,
rising from the canals,
or the tin ship lights
of the East Coast Grill,
in Boston,
hung above the bar
inviting those there
to float past Cambridge
to see Harvard Square
in the dark,
full of music and laughter,

like the songs of the heron
in the tall marsh grass
of Japan,
with its long stick legs
and red-crowned head,
as tall as a man
in the land
of the silent gongs,
that soothe the soul
with a sound that surrounds,
like that sound from the ground
as the waves hit the shore,
when the ocean lands
in rhythmic bands of color
and the sun sets
on the deep green forests
of Vancouver,
or the dry, purple mountains
of Arizona deserts,
and the white sands of Miami
        Beach,
next to pink flamingo
        hotels,
where the sun warms the
        palms
and the mind relaxes,
drifting in time
with the waves of comfort,
just as drifting up now,
toward the surface,
returning to this place,
this time,
returning to wakeful
        awareness,
where the eyes open,
and so does the mind,
alert and rested,
comfortable and awake,

eyes open **now.**   eyes open
That's right,   and wide awake now.

FLOATING FREE

A Basic Induction and Reorientation Script.

So,
close your eyes now,
and we will take some time,
whatever time you need,
to learn how it feels
to relax even more,
to let go
of the effort it takes
to hold on
and to try
to pay close attention
to all those sensations,
thoughts, images, perhaps,
that dance through the mind,
float past awareness,
even though there is no need
to make an effort
to hold on, now,
no need to do anything at all
except allow
the mind to drift
anywhere at all,
the way milkweed seeds,
tiny bits of fluff,
drift up on the wind,
carried from here to there,
floating free of everywhere,
the seeds of a thought
that begin to form,

then drift away,
carried on a breeze
with the gentle lightness
of being,
being able to drift free,
down toward that feeling
of effortless letting go,
and going along,
as light as a song,
floating on the still, calm air,
floating anywhere at all,
free from it all,
where the mind drifts free,
like the dry fall leaves,
full of color and sun,
yet each and every one
catches the breeze
as it falls from the trees
and floats off,
a butterfly wing of color
toward a different place,
floats off toward a different
     space,
and you can drift as well,
easily, gently, quietly,
drifting down,
down toward that sound,
that silent sound
of the mind going down,

the mind floating down,
allowing your unconscious
        mind
to carry you along,
along toward a comfortable
        place,
a silent, restful place
of peaceful self-awareness,
where you are free to see,
to hear and feel,
free to be
anything at all,
that inner place,
where you become aware
of letting go,
of going on,
in your own time,
in your own way,
on into that trance,
that gentle dance
that transforms the mind
and smoothes the flow
as you continue to go
down, and deeper,
until you begin to know

how it feels below,
in that safe, secure
place to be,
relaxed and able
to allow the mind
to drift free in its own
        time,
to see and do things
that otherwise might be
difficult
or confusing,
but now turn out to be
        easier
and easier,
just as drifting up
becomes easier now,
just as waking up
is comfortable now,
having learned to allow
a trance state of mind,
you can find
the mind waking,
the eyes opening,
and wakefulness returning,
now.

COHORTS

A Basic Induction

It is so easy
to be even more comfortable
now,
allowing the chair
to support the spine,
the legs, the shoulders,
as you observe your breathing,
slowly making it deeper and
    deeper,
taking long, slow breaths,
you follow that breath,
flowing through the spine
to its base and returning
to the crown of the head
as you **exhale,** that's right.
And as you continue to follow
your breath to find
that depth of trance you desire,
your conscious mind can enjoy
the things I say as your
unconscious mind employs
its own understandings.
Now, psychologists who study
human development
have long noted
that people who are born
in the same decade
share common ideas,
common values and memories,
and these shared ideas are so
    strong
we refer to age-mates

as cohort groups.
And I can't help but wonder
what specific memories,
ideas, and sensations
will take you back
to your early days.
If you were born in the 1930s,
you would remember President
    Roosevelt,
and Bonnie and Clyde,
and maybe your parents
had hard times
in the Depression,
but you survived,
but if you were born in the
    1940s,
you probably enjoy the "Big
    Band" sound
and maybe you saved paper
    and tin
because a war was on,
and remember Betty Grable
    and
a young Frank Sinatra.
And if you were born in the
    1950s,
you may remember Howdy
    Doody
and eating TV dinners
and loving Lucy.
Did you dance the jitterbug
or can you recall

a few more verses
of that Elvis Presley song?
And songs unleash the 1960s,
so many songs—of peace
and protest,
the Viet Nam war,
the freedom march,
became a way of life.
Amazing what the mind makes
   out
of its pictures and memories,
of straight hair
and painted faces,
of signs carried
and "flower power,"
and where were you that day
President Kennedy was shot?
And if you were born in the
   1970s,
leisure was well suited
to the times,
the Beatles still together,
but soon separate,
and while you played Atari,

your parents wondered
about the missing 18 minutes
or who shot J.R.
And you can wonder as well
about the mind's ability
to head back to where we've
   been,
as though the future were hidden somewhere
in the carnival of events
we call our memories.
So while you lie there,
in the chair,
you can feel
the golden cord
that reaches back
and links you to
your special time and place,
a place of quiet comfort
and genuine delights,
while that same cord
leads you forward,
to whatever the future
brings you to.

(May be followed by therapeutic metaphors or reorientation suggestions.)

WARP AND WOOF

A Confusion Induction for Subjects Who Find Trance Difficult to Experience

And as you begin to relax,
with your eyes closed,
preparing to enter trance
without knowing
what that is feeling like,
many thoughts and sensations
run through the mind,
weaving a variety
of different feelings,
a variety
of different experiences,
going back and forth
like the threads of a weaver
weaving a rug on a loom,
sitting in that room,
different colors of yarn,
spinning a yarn
about things that loom
far off in the distance,
coming closer all the time,
back and forth goes the yarn,
so many different colors,
up and then down,
this time across that way,
next time a cross of gray,
perhaps with a red or a brown,
a brown yarn,
like a tall tale,
spun from the tail of a lion,
lying on the ground
all around,

those colors spun
on a wheel,
and spinning
twists them up,
makes them dizzy
to consider the height,
the height of the rug
beneath the carpet,
up one side
and down the other,
not knowing if coming or going
together
is going to be
what it is all about,
as the spinning yarn continues
to unravel and fall apart,
just as the tall tail
of the white-tailed deer
stands up
as it runs about,
springs about as it leaps
in the spring,
a spring in its step
as you try to step
closer to see the strings
that move back and forth
to weave that song
on the old guitar,
that seems to be one thing,
but turns out to have been
nothing at all,

just like the weaver said,
before the thoughts began,
before all thought began
it was so much easier
to just relax,
aware of those things
that occur along the way,
but not needing
to weigh the difference
to see if it is OK
to just let go
and go on your way,
staying there

in that trance there,
where you rest
and wait
and wonder
what pleasant thing
will weave into your thoughts
as you relax even more,
        now,
and continue drifting down,
        now,
down even more than before
into that deep, comfortable
trance.

(*May be followed by additional metaphors or a reorientation to wakefulness.*)

A CHILD'S SLIDE

An Autohypnosis Training Induction

Holding on is one thing,
and letting go is another,
and you already know
how to hold on,
how to hold on to awareness
of a hand resting there,
or a leg relaxing there,
holding on to the thoughts,
the curious wonderings
of what will happen next,
or if what went before
was a trance or not
really doesn't matter any more,
because now you can begin
to continue letting go,
letting go of the effort

to pay close attention
to anything special at all,
discovering how it feels
to let go of it all
and to feel the mind fall,
in a gentle, drifting way
all the way down,
down to the ground,
sliding down effortlessly,
just the way a child slides
        down,
down that thing called a slide,
being at the top
and letting go,
sliding down,
effortlessly pulled down,

and all you need to do
is nothing at all,
just drifting down,
gliding smoothly down,
enjoying the ride
all the way down,
then resting there,
looking up at the sky,
the silent sigh of joy inside,
the pleasure of that feeling
of going down that way,
and then climbing back,
up to the top,
drifting back up
to normal, wakeful awareness
already,
ready to look around
to hear the sounds
and feel the feelings
of wakeful alertness
as the mind returns,
and then ready to let go
again,
ready to allow
that drifting down again,
deeper this time,
perhaps,
more quickly this time,
perhaps,
recognizing that feeling,
that feeling of letting go,
returning to that peaceful
    calm,
allowing the mind to slide
    down,
to drift gently down deeper
    inside,
down and down some more,

and then back up again,
back toward the surface again,
back awake again,
as the unconscious mind
reminds the mind
that the hands are here,
that the legs are there,
that you are here,
and then,
just when
it seems to you
that you are almost there,
almost awake again,
you can recall that feeling,
remember that experience,
of letting go
and drifting down,
down with the sound
of my voice,
down with the effortless ease,
floating down that slide again,
following that path within,
drifting down inside the mind,
returning to that place inside,
learning even more than before
how easy it is to return,
to drift in,
to drift down,
to allow the unconscious
    mind
to assume more and more
responsibility
for doing those things needed,
while deep inside,
the mind relaxes,
finds a place to be,
and enjoys the ride
back up outside,

knowing now how
to return there again
anytime at all,
anytime you wish,
anytime you need,
to be able to drift up
now,
to return to wakeful alertness,
now,
having learned how

to do this for you,
to relax for you,
and wake up too,
just as you wake up now,
eyes open,
mind alert and rested,
wide awake now.
That's right.
That's right.
Wide awake.

AEROBICS INSTRUCTORS

An Induction for Responsive Subjects

But don't begin
too soon
to drift down into that trance,
or do it too fast.
Take your time, now,
to give your unconscious a
    chance
to find the rhythm
and remember the feeling
of drifting down within,
the way people watch the
    instructor
in an aerobics class,
following along
each movement,
watching how to move
arms, legs, and feet,
and doing exactly what
the instructor says,
lost in the words
and in the beat

as they just let go
and let their body do
what it is told to do,
just as you can, too,
listening and watching
that instructor in your mind,
your unconscious instructor,
showing you what to do,
showing you how it feels
to feel that trance,
to allow that trance
to develop in you,
to feel the changes
in arms and legs,
the changes in how you think
and feel,
as your unconscious mind
instructs and leads,
and you it,
toward that trance,
doing that trance

dance,
until your conscious mind
lets go completely,
and the unconscious mind
finds it easier and easier
to understand my words
and meanings,
and to help you
understand them too,
even without knowing
that you do,
and do what you know
you are supposed to do,
as you learn even more
about what you know,
and what you
need to do
to take care
of you
as you drift
deep into
that trance state
now,
and deeper,
knowing how
to let go now
and listen to
the rest of the story,
that's right. . . .

(May be followed by therapeutic metaphors or a few trance termination comments.)

NOW HEAR THIS

Brief Inductions for Experienced Subjects

1.

Relaxing,
letting go now,
returning to that place,
to that deep trance place,
where all effort drifts away,
and events occur
almost automatically.
That's right,
take your own time
to allow that feeling
to return.

2.

With your eyes closed again,
listening
to the sound of my voice, again,
drifting down once more,
where you have been before,
and can enjoy
returning there
now.

3.

Now,
with your eyes closed,
you can drift into a trance,
drifting down again,
letting go again,
remembering
and reexperiencing
that feeling,
that way of being,
that way of allowing
thoughts
and sensations
to happen
automatically.

4.

That's right,
so comfortable
to not need
to make the effort it takes
to do anything at all,
just letting go
and becoming
quietly entranced
by those things
that happen
along the way.

(May be followed by metaphorical anecdotes such as those presented in later chapters.)

5

IMAGINARY RESOURCES

The vivid imagination of a child can place monsters under the bed or transform a living room into a spaceship. These imagined monsters can trigger the same reactions that they would if they were real. Furthermore, a child's behavior, thinking, and personality may change dramatically when he or she enters into the role of captain aboard that imagined spaceship. A new repertoire of actions and reactions emerges and that child seems to becomes a different person for a brief time. There is a thin curtain between imagined events and real ones, between who we imagine ourselves to be and who we are. It is such a translucent veil that imagined scenes can have significant long-term physiological, cognitive, and behavioral consequences.

Everyone has heard the maxim, "Practice makes perfect." This old saying suggests, quite rightly, that mastery of a new skill or the development of a new habit requires rehearsal. What this old saying fails to acknowledge, however, is that such practice can be imagined rather that actual. Learning does occur in response to imagined scenes and imagined rehearsal sessions. Our ability to learn as a result of imagined scenes is the basis for the covert conditioning procedures developed by Cautela (1966, 1967, 1973) and Wolpe (1969). During these procedures, people imagine themselves engaging in some act and then imagine either a pleasantly rewarding outcome or an unpleasant outcome. The imagined behavior is thereby either rewarded and made more likely to occur in real life or punished and made less likely to occur.

Lazarus (1984) took this approach one step further by describing the benefits of the imagined practice of new behaviors, such as assertiveness and physical performance. Significant improvements in performance take place following the imagined rehearsal of athletic performances, musical performances, sexual activities, and positive interpersonal styles. In addition, when people imagine how they would behave and feel if they had different mental sets, they find it easier to change their attitudes, schemas, and responses in the imagined direction.

Imagined events can alter patterns of learning and response to external situations, and they can modify attitudes and beliefs, as well. Research also suggests that imagined events have an impact on physiological states. Simonton and Matthews-Simonton (1978), for example, suggested that visual imagery could be used to stimulate the body's natural defenses in the fight against cancer. Such claims may seem to be extreme, but studies such as those by Crawford (1985), Rider and Achterberg (1989), Rider et al. (1990), and Smith, Schneider, Minning, and Whitcher (1983) have consistently found significant increases in specific immune system functions when subjects are asked to imagine such improvements. Rossi (1986) suggested a model of the specific neural pathways that translate such imagined events into physiological responses at the endocrine, neurotransmitter, and immune system levels. Rossi also suggested that the mind/body connection is so pronounced that virtually any physiological function or response can be influenced by mind-generated thoughts and images, though these responses are not always capable of overcoming specific disease processes (cf. Taylor, 1989).

Efforts to use imagined events to improve learning, mental sets, or physiological responses typically employ progressive relaxation training or soothing music to enhance relaxation and imagery. This work also has concentrated almost exclusively on visual imagery and has often ignored the potential impact of imaginative involvement in our other sensory modalities, such as smell, hearing, and taste.

The focused attention and absorption of hypnotic trance allow us to take the power of imaginary resources beyond the use of ordinary visual imagery. Trance can be used to generate an intense, effortless, or involuntary participation in imagined events, a participation that includes all of the sights, sounds, sensations, and feelings associated with that event (cf. Kroger & Fezler, 1976). Indeed, such experiences are the hallmark of hypnosis, and they may even be responsible for many of the phenomena typically associated with it (cf. Fromm & Shor, 1979). The hypnotic experience becomes so all-encompassing and vivid that it actually seems "real" (Hilgard (1965). While completely immersed in these imagined scenes, clients can practice new response patterns and rehearse new skills or sharpen old ones. They can try out new mental sets or seek to alter physiological functions. The lively, multimodal intensity of a hypnotic experience reportedly strengthens and extends the therapeutic effect of imagined events (cf. Hilgard, 1979; Kroger & Fezler, 1976).

The following scripts work to establish a client's ability to become intensely involved in imagined experiences. This ability then can be used either by the therapist to present a particular imaginary scene that is directly or symbolically relevant to that individual's goals, needs, and interests, or by the individual to "try out" new responses and to rehearse particular skills. Many of the metaphorical anecdotes in the scripts presented in the following chapters utilize this hypnotically intensified imaginative involvement to stimulate new learnings and response tendencies.

INNER REALITIES

A Trance to Stimulate Imagination

And do you relax,
as you sit back in your seat,
waiting for the movie to start?
Not knowing
what to expect,
as the lights go dark,
and the curtains part,
and the screen begins to glow,
and images appear,
flashing lights and sound
that surround the mind
with the question
of what comes next,
like the darting lights
that dance in the mind,
with the eyes closed
behind their lids,
watching those colors form
and arrange themselves
in cells and forms
that emerge on their own,
just as if
there are flashing, dancing
lights out there,
flashing in those patterns
right before your eyes,
starburst surprises
like fireworks,
or were they fireflies
on that day,
when you walked into that
    house

and took a deep breath
and smelled that aroma,
that rich, wonderful smell,
that made you feel so happy
that it surprises you now
and lets you know
what day it was,
or where you are,
as you sat down there,
and felt that feeling
that place provides,
deep down inside
the sounds and smells,
the tastes yet to come,
as the guests arrive
and talk begins
to surround the mind
with that knowing where
    you've been
and not knowing
where you are going
to go
or what to do there then,
when the movie starts
and you feel yourself
float out of your seat
into that screen
becoming that person there,
seeing those things
in that scene,
and beginning to do
what you need to do,

as your unconscious mind
constructs for you
an ability
to enter that place,
an ability
to hear those sounds,
an ability
to move around there,
to taste and smell
the flavors of the wind,
and to know your body knows
how it feels
to do those things,
as you realize now,
that you do know how
to go anywhere,
anytime,
to see and feel and do
whatever you wish
to be or do,
whatever it is
you want to do,
can be done in there,
in the inner spaces,
those private places,

just as real as real,
and you can feel
that knowing now growing,
becoming an ability
you can use,
returning to those movies,
the movies of the mind,
that let you do anything
at the time,
to see and feel,
to try out how
to do those things
you need to now,
and when you know you can,
you can feel yourself
drifting back,
out of there to here,
back to comfortable,
wakeful awareness,
where the eyes
almost seem to open
by themselves.
That's right,
eyes open
and wide **awake now**.

(*This session is followed by a brief interview to determine the vividness of the various sensory events mentioned during the trance.*)

DISTANT SHORES

A Trance to Stimulate Imaginative Involvement

Each night
you dream,
and in those dreams
you walk,
you talk,
you look at things,
you feel things,
and as you relax,
here and now,
you can continue
to feel yourself
drifting into a dream,
experiencing another place,
another time,
even more clearly, perhaps,
than you have before,
as you walked along that shore
where the warm sunlight
        danced
and threw bright sparkles
into your eyes,
and you could smell
the sweet water,
a fresh, alive smell,
as the wind brushes the skin
now and then,
and the rhythmic sounds of the
        waves,
that gentle rushing in,
captures the mind,
and soothes it deep down,
looking as you walk

where your feet step soft,
and you see those things,
here and there along the shore,
small and large, rough and
        smooth,
washed up by the waves
that still wash in
to bring a cool wetness
now and then to each step;
a refreshing walk,
as the muscles in each leg
remember and feel
the tired heaviness
of that exercise,
that stepping along,
along with that feeling inside,
that quiet connection,
to the colors of the shore,
the songs and cries of the
        birds,
and are there people there,
laughing or playing,
or is it silent now,
only you there,
walking,
thinking,
looking,
feeling,
and aware of being
peaceful inside,
not thinking about that ride
to get where you are,

in a bus
or a car,
or was it a plane,
is it that far
away,
or do you
come here often,
to walk this shore,
to hear those sounds,
to see those things
you are now
able to experience
quite clearly,
able to allow,
able to enjoy,
even now
as you begin to drift
        back,

back to the here and now,
back to this room,
away from that shore,
knowing you can allow yourself
to drift into anyplace,
any image and experience,
anytime you want or need
to do so,
just as you did now,
while you gradually reach that
        point
where the mind begins
to awaken,
to come back into here,
and the eyes
seem ready to open,
almost by themselves,
right now.

6

OPTIMISM

Optimism is a vital ingredient of physical and mental wellness. The presence or absence of optimism can predict one's level of depression, coping skills, and potential for disease (for reviews see Dillon, Minchoff, & Baker, 1985; Ornstein & Sobel, 1989; Peterson & Bossio, 1991; Seligman, 1990). Negativity of attitude or idea is neither healthy nor productive, even when such attitudes are objectively accurate. However, positive beliefs and attitudes will enhance happiness, even when such beliefs are not entirely accurate (cf. Lockard & Paulhus, 1988).

Thus believing our physical health to be good or excellent, when it is only poor to fair, may actually enhance our health, whereas stoically facing and resigning ourselves to the bad news about our health may have negative consequences (Kaplan & Comacho, 1983; Lazarus, 1979). In a similar vein, it appears that believing we have some personal control over our life situations, even those situations where little actual control is possible, will enhance both our self-esteem and our ability to cope with change (Kobasa, Maddi, & Kahn, 1982; Phares, 1976; Schier & Carver, 1985).

In the past decade, three distinct lines of research have provided evidence for the beneficial effects of optimism. First, as researchers in cognitive psychology began to document the various ways people think about themselves and the world, they were confronted by the cognitive implications of optimistic interpretations and mental sets (Taylor, 1989). Optimism enhances problem

solving and competence. Second, research on depression suggested that optimism provides a buffer against depression
(Abramson & Alloy, 1981; Alloy, Abramson, & Viscusi, 1981).
Third, medical and psychological research revealed that optimism
about one's health actually enhances health (Kaplan & Camacho,
1983), and that optimism in general appears to improve behavior
in a healthy direction and to enhance the function of the immune
system as well (Bandura, Taylor, Williams, Mefford, & Barchas,
1985; Kiecolt-Glaser & Glaser, 1988; Wallston & Wallston, 1982).

The healing characteristics of optimism have been delineated
in the literature. But healthy optimism is more than a vague
notion that things will always turn out for the best. Rather, "effective optimism" (Epstein & Meier, 1989) is grounded in three basic
beliefs: (1) a positive view of the self; (2) a belief that one can exert
control over one's life; and (3) a belief that life is meaningful. These
are the "positive illusions" (Taylor, 1989) of the optimist. Positive
expectations, proactivity, and personal meaning all interact to create a more psychologically healthy and hardy human being
(Kobasa et al., 1882).

What follows are scripts that acknowledge the benefits of optimism. Initially, the themes of optimism may be elusive for both
client and clinician. Many professionals have become skilled in pessimism and skepticism. Until recently, optimism was considered
to be intellectually unfashionable. Schooled in the pessimism of
Freud and behaviorism, many of us struggle with optimism as the
basis of a new psychological paradigm. Here and elsewhere we
must remind ourselves, as Erickson often did, that what we are
trained to see is not, by any means, all there is. Erickson frequently quoted the biblical saying, "As a man believeth in his
heart, so he is." When people believe in themselves, in their ability
to control events, and in the meaningfulness of their lives, so it
is.

DEFENDING YOUR LIFE

An Entrancing Introduction to Optimism

And as we begin today,
your conscious mind can begin
to affirm your self-worth,
as your unconscious mind
    guides
your ability to express your
    needs
in a positive and effective way,
and I don't know,
and you don't know,
exactly how
this expression may occur.
Perhaps it will begin
with a relaxation
of the muscles of the forehead,
or a feeling of comfort and
    contentment
that you can associate with
    self-acceptance,
and the limitless potentials
the unconscious mind provides.
As you rest there
in the chair,
and become aware
of all the possibilities
available to you,
you may wish to begin
to release all judgments,
all negative thoughts,
all critical feelings,
though I wouldn't want
you to do this completely.

right now,
so much easier
to let go of fear
and criticism
in your own time,
in your own way,
and your conscious mind
can reassure you,
as your unconscious mind
    reaches deep
within your spirit,
to retrieve those feelings
    of
support, love, creativity,
which are the world to you.
Now, optimistic points of view
are not always in fashion,
as the movie critic
often makes clear,
rating films highly
that deal with ruthless
    alienation,
but if it is about hope or
    compassion,
finding it saccharine,
    sentimental,
as if only helpless sadness is
    real.
But reality is only a story
we tell ourselves
and so why not enjoy
the happy endings,

the hopeful scenarios
in the movies of our own lives,
for people, it seems,
have a natural inclination,
from childhood on,
to believe that good things
will happen,
and when you believe
you can make good things
    happen,
the chances of happiness are
    higher,
because they do,
so, even if life deals the deck,
you can always play
the percentages
that roll in your favor,
taking control of moods,
of thoughts,
demanding a room with a view,
windows opening wide
to the fullness of life.
There is a movie, a comedy,
about a man who, after dying,
ended up in the next best place
to heaven,
where he was to stay
until he could defend his life
by demonstrating how often
he had lived without fear,
how often he had accepted
    risks,
faced challenges,
sought love and appreciated
    beauty,
without fear,
felt content with himself,
without fear,

because he could not move on,
evolve,
take his place in the next
    world,
until he proved he did these
    things,
and you know
when you first learned to walk,
you did it without fear,
it didn't matter if you fell down,
you got up,
without being mad at yourself,
and if you had worried
about perfect penmanship
at age 5 or 6,
you would not be able
to write your name today.
Keeping the critic
alive inside us
only subdues the spirit,
and makes us miss what is real,
so go ahead, why not be
too open to experience,
why not love too much,
yourself and others,
why not be eccentrically you,
why not believe in hope,
and know compassion,
and feel beauty,
being excessively happy.
You can wear the drab
    camouflage
of pessimism,
and make life a war movie,
at war with yourself,
but imagining the color purple
may be more useful
when it comes to

defending your life,
now or a few moments from
    now
as you begin to drift back

to wakeful awareness
of what you are aware of,
and how you do it
now.

ERICKSON'S OPTIMISM

A Trance to Develop Optimism

Now, Milton Erickson was an
    optimist
who knew a lot
about putting people in charge
of their lives
and he believed in actions
speaking louder than
    intentions,
so it does not surprise me at all
when I hear stories
about the ways he motivated
his clients to change.
And you can decide
whether you're surprised
or not as you listen,
comfortably,
to the stories I tell
about an alcoholic man,
who came to see Erickson,
and told Dr. Erickson how
    much
he wished to quit drinking
and how every day he left his
    house
full of good intentions
but on his way to work,
a walk of one mile,

he passed a beer garden
and he couldn't walk by
without stopping for a drink,
and he couldn't take the bus
because he'd get off for a beer.
And Erickson told him
some streets he could take to
    work,
streets with no beer gardens,
and the distance would be six
    miles,
and he said, "it's a good,
    healthy walk,
for a broken-down alcoholic
full of good resolves."
And the man walked six miles
to work and back each day,
and he stopped drinking,
and learned to zigzag
across streets so he'd never
walk in front of a beer garden,
and then he learned he was a
    free man
who could walk
down any street he wished.
And I'm wondering now
if it would surprise you

to discover that Dr. Erickson
had ways of turning
people's negative emotions
about themselves
into more positive feelings,
like the time a little girl
came to see him.
She was 8 years old,
and her face was covered
with freckles
and she hated
every one of those freckles,
she hated her mother, her
    father,
the milkman, her teacher,
she hated herself,
and everyone else.
She even hated her
    grandparents
from Kansas,
whom she'd never even met,
all because she hated her
    freckles.
Dr. Erickson met her
and accused her
of stealing,
he told her she was a thief
and that he knew
what she had stolen
and from where.
This made her quite furious,
to be accused of stealing,
until Dr. Erickson told her
what she had stolen, and
    where.
She was in the kitchen,
sneaking in the cookie jar,
full of cinnamon cookies,

cinnamon buns,
and cinnamon rolls,
and while filching from
the cookie jar,
she spilled cinnamon
all over her face . . .
she was a cinnamon face!
Now, the girl was quite
    relieved,
and liked it that her freckles
were special,
he gave her freckles a new
    name . . .
a cinnamon face is a face you can
be proud of.
Dr. Erickson understood
    nature
and recognized that it's our
    differences
that make us beautiful and
    special,
and the solutions to our
    difficulties
are always within our reach,
just like handfuls of cinnamon
    cookies,
as long as we are willing
to go the distance
it takes to get in charge
and like ourselves for what we
    are,
like you can now,
drifting up
into the silent recognition
that you own cinnamon
    speckles
of a different color
that are just as sweet.

ROSE-COLORED GLASSES

A Trance to Develop Optimism

At one time
or another,
everyone eventually
gets their eyes checked
to see if they can see,
or if what they see
is a clear reflection
of what is really there,
and so they sit there
and read the letters
arranged upon that chart,
and then look through
the different lenses
that alter and distort,
until the optometrist decides
what is the matter
with their vision
and prescribes special lenses
that straighten
everything right out.
But what about the mind,
and the way it can change
the way we see
or what we see
and how we see things there
out in the world
and in our lives
where it would be quite rare
for things to be
the way we want,
things cooked exactly right,
not too rare,

and not too sweet,
everything all right,
not left behind
not far ahead,
but in our heads
just the way
we always wanted them to be
would be a strange event
indeed,
because we always can want
     more
or wish that they were
     different,
and certainly
have the capacity
to expect things to go wrong,
or to see something wrong
in whatever way things are,
thinking it would be bizarre
for the bazaar of life to offer
things that meet our every
     need
and always turn out right
like little John,
a small person,
a one-time hood,
who always knew
that everything was hard,
that nothing worked out right,
that life is full of terrors
that linger in the night
and filled his head

with memories and dreams
of lessons learned before
and angry rages
filled with fury
from a father
who never understood
and who yelled at him
from dusk to dawn,
no matter how hard he tried
to make things turn out right
and so he worked hard
just to stay afloat,
fighting with the flow
of each of life's events,
being angry and upset
whenever things went wrong
as he always expected them to,
and they always seemed to,
proud that he knew
that life is out of joint,
always something wrong,
not perfect,
that was his only point,
and proud of being able
to find something terrible
about everything that
          happened,
always expecting the worst,
and getting it,
left him quite exhausted
with all his complaining
until one day
his heart stood still
for just a little while,
and let him know
that this was not the way
to enjoy himself or others
without the tiniest of smiles,

and that even if it meant
it would be
crazy and/or stupid
the time had come
for him to find
a pleasant state of being
where things looked bright
and tastes were right
and people were worth seeing
as gentle souls
who wished him well
and life would turn out right,
always full of opportunities
to learn and to enjoy
the things that he had lost
as a tiny boy
and now could find
in a raindrop,
or a sunset,
each full of colors and promise
of a new day in the morning
where flowers grow
and spread their scent
in honey on the wind,
and even though a tire
goes flat
or the car stops still
or someone makes an error,
there always is the opportunity
to use that chance
to find a friend
or to discover something new
that otherwise might have
          gone
overlooked,
a place to stop
and see the view,
a different point of view

where things seem fine
just the way they are
and all will turn out right
eventually,
the way they say
the yin and yang
are always in
perfect harmony,
balancing each other out,
where every danger and
    unhappiness
is also an opportunity
to take advantage of,
to turn life around
and seize the sour moment
to make some lemonade,
because, as every small child
    knows,
where there is manure,
there must be a pony
    somewhere,
or like the man who was told
that he had a deadly disease
and so he stopped and looked
    around
and decided to change his life
to have some fun
and to see in each moment
an opportunity
to feel good about himself
and to know
that things would turn out
    right
in the end,
and that was many years ago
and he is still doing that,
planning the brightest futures
he can find,

planning them carefully in his
    mind
and seeing every moment
as an opportunity
to let the wonders of the world
unfold before his eyes,
knowing it is just as easy
to always expect the best
and to enjoy the rest
from working so hard,
just as you can now,
resting easily
and effortlessly able to imagine
how it will be
to allow yourself to break free
and to astonish others
with your ability
to see the possibilities,
the endless opportunities
in everything that happens
and everything that is,
because what is
is just what is,
but what you do with what
    is
is entirely up to you.
To allow that change
to occur
at the deepest level
of your being,
and give your unconscious
    mind
permission to go on seeing
images of opportunities
and how to best utilize
whatever there is there
anywhere and anytime
and permission to give

those understandings and
     ideas
to you,
and to keep on doing so
even as you begin
to drift up toward the surface
now,
up to the surface of wakeful
     alertness

now,
feeling wide awake and
     refreshed
now,
even as the mind drifts up,
and the eyes open
as wakefulness returns
now. . . .

7

FRIENDS AND LOVERS

"People who need people are the luckiest people in the world," says the song, and recent research seems to bear this out. Social interactions with family, friends, loved ones, and even a treasured pet apparently contribute to health and happiness. People with strong social ties live longer, get sick less often, and recover from sickness more rapidly and with fewer complications than do those who are socially isolated (House, Landis, & Umberson, 1988; Schaefer, Coyne, & Lazarus, 1981). They also experience a more positive sense of well-being than their isolated peers (Wallston & Wallston, 1982).

The influences of interpersonal relationships on physical and emotional life are complex. Suffice it to say that the evidence supporting the link between social support and health is so well documented that the term "psychosocial risk" has been coined to describe the impact of social isolation (Smilkstein, 1988). When assessing an individual's overall risk for disease, psychosocial risk is included with the other factors traditionally recognized as contributing to poor health, such as smoking, drinking, and high stress. Isolation, loneliness, and low social support are hazardous to the health of the mind and body. On the other hand, connectedness, a sense of being related or connected to others, appears to be vital to wellness.

It is worth noting that this emphasis on connectedness flies in the face of many contemporary psychological theories of growth and development. Although theorists such as Fromm (1941) and Sullivan (1953) emphasized the importance of interpersonal and social involvement throughout the 1940s and 1950s, more recent authors typically have emphasized the importance of individuation and autonomy as the path toward maturity (cf. Erikson, 1963, 1968; Mahler, Pine, & Berman, 1975; Levinson, 1978). It probably is fair to say that recent American cultural values also stress "becoming one's own man," as Levinson puts it.

In light of our American belief in "rugged individualism" and self-reliance, the research comparing the Japanese and Americans on the dimensions of health and social connectedness is especially striking. Japan and the United States are well matched in terms of such variables as industrialization, urbanization, high stress, and quick pace, but the Japanese have a much lower rate of heart disease and higher life expectancy than do Americans (Marmot, Syme, Kagan, Kats, Cohen, & Belsky, 1975). This health advantage seems to hold, however, only for those Japanese who live in Japan. Japanese immigrants in the United States quickly lose this edge on health. Their rate of heart disease, for example, parallels that of other Americans. What is the explanation for this? Follow-up research by Marmot and Syme (1976) suggests that it is the highly connected, cooperative nature of traditional Japanese social networks that provides a disease buffer. The loss of these networks actually jeopardizes health. This hypothesis is supported by the finding that Japanese immigrants who maintain traditional kinship and social networks demonstrate the same longevity and lack of heart problems as do their counterparts in Japan, whereas immigrants who have assimilated American social isolationism show elevated rates of heart disease and shorter life expectancies. These findings persist when all other risk factors, including diet, smoking, and stress, are taken into account. Clearly, it may be wise for Americans to reconsider the cultural imperatives that isolate us from each other and lead us to believe that we should rely only on ourselves.

A sense of connectedness or social involvement is not the only aspect of our interpersonal lives that contributes to our health and well-being. Altruism, or doing good deeds for others, also seems to be beneficial for our overall wellness. People who help others, who give their time and resources to people they may not even know, have increased life expectancies as compared with their more selfish counterparts (cf. Growald & Luks, 1988; Luks, 1988). Luks (1988), for example, reported that many people experience emotional and physical changes characteristic of an "exercise high" when they engage in helping others. Doing good deeds is good for us, and it feels good too.

Connectedness and altruism involve empathy, caring, and a sense of involvement in the lives of others. Feminist therapists have frequently questioned the popular notion that separation from others is a hallmark of psychological growth and that loving others is a symptom of pathology (e.g., Gilligan, 1982; Surrey, 1991; Walters, 1988a). It now appears that their objections have considerable empirical support.

The trance sessions in this chapter are devoted to an internal exploration of the benefits of cooperation, mutuality, and connectedness. They encourage each individual to experience the benefits of broadening his or her social network. Emphasis is placed on empathic communication, altruism, and the creation of interpersonal connections.

HEART TO HEART

A Trance to Encourage Connectedness

Your conscious mind is waiting
to depart,
as your unconscious checks
to be sure
you'll be taking everything
you need for the journey,
and it is nice to know
you can cross that bridge, now,
or when you come to it,
your breath rising and falling,
the mind rising and falling,
in harmony
with the breath,
and the heart beating,
      rhythmically,
comfortably open
to a new awareness.
And once I heard
of a hypnotist
who used a metronome
as part of a trance induction,
and I wonder
if she recognized
that the sound of a metronome
mirrors the meter of
the heartbeat,
and certainly provides
a very familiar
sense of security,
as well as reminding us
that the heart is a metaphor
everyone understands.

Its beat meters life,
it is our favorite symbol
of love.
The tin man longed
for one of his own,
favored reservoir of affection,
love, passion, connection,
every heartbeat
bears your name,
loud and clear
it stakes its claim,
is only one song,
one in a million,
about the heart
and its devotions.
So it is not surprising
how our heart goes out to
those held hostage
in foreign lands,
because the real ordeal
is the isolation,
the loss of friends,
the loss of community.
"I am very lonely,"
Terry Anderson said
on videotape,
and later spoke
of teaching sign language
to his fellow hostages,
so even in isolation,
when speaking was not
      allowed,

their hands reached through
    bars
to speak to each other,
to stay connected together.
Humans are social animals,
and silent disconnection
holds the heart hostage.
Milton Erickson often told his
    clients
to give a gift to someone
or ask another for help,
knowing that being apart
from others
was hazardous to your
    health
and to your happiness,
because affection,
and connection,
anchor the drifting heart,

and hearts beat stronger,
and last longer,
when we love.
Even pets shift our hearts
outside ourselves,
and connect us
to a larger world,
where Dorothy risked her
    safety
to save her puppy, Toto,
and the tin man earns his
    heart
when he discovers he has
    always known
how to love,
and you earn your heart as
    well,
when you open it
to others.

SOCIAL SECURITY

A Trance for Teaching Altruism

As your conscious mind
considers what you're doing,
your unconscious mind is
    interested
in being
comfortable and learning
something new and satisfying,
and real time
is a scarce commodity,
but trance time
is all the time in the world
to learn,

so take your time to drift
    down,
because you have so much time
to give yourself
the things you need,
and as you drift, my words
will be about the boon
of giving to others, as well,
in a healthy fashion.
Now, in childhood,
you learned to always take a
    friend

with you
whenever you went swimming
so she would be there for you
in times of trouble or danger,
so the unconscious mind
looks out for you here now.
And it is interesting to dis-
     cover how
the "buddy system" works
in other ways, as well.
For just as being taken care of
fills us with security,
taking care of others
may provide us with security
     as well.
In certain experiments
researchers have discovered
the "high" of helping,
discovered that people feel
a rush, a euphoria,
when they reach out to others,
and that older persons live
     longer,
are healthier when they do
volunteer work,
and helping strangers is
     particularly
gratifying
for everyone.
Now, Milton Erickson
was a compassionate man,
and a competent therapist,
who filled his life
with friends and family,
which is probably how he
     developed
his "pain calluses,"
because he had polio

twice in his life,
and he taught himself to walk
twice in his life,
so he knew about pain,
which is probably how he knew
to tell a construction worker,
paralyzed in a fall,
how he could develop
calluses on his nerves too,
and he told this man
to ask his friends to bring him
cartoons and comics
and funny stories,
which he should collect
and paste into scrapbooks,
and when one of his
fellow workers
was ill or had an accident,
he told the paralyzed man
to send his friend a scrapbook,
and he made hundreds of
     scrapbooks,
and he felt much better.
Erickson was wise,
he understood the social body.
He liked to tell the story of
a lonely, depressed woman,
with all the money in the world
but no friends
and no family.
She read the Bible
and went to church,
but never talked to anyone
or lingered afterwards
for tea and company,
and her maids and
her housekeepers took care
of all her needs

as she sat alone
in her big house,
becoming more despondent
    every day.
So, Dr. Erickson paid her a
    visit
and saw she could grow
African violets,
which are quite fragile
and require lots of loving care.
Even a little neglect
can kill them.
And when he saw those deli-
    cate violets,
he gave the woman medical
    orders
to send her housekeeper
to the florist to buy violets
in every shade and color that
    existed,
and to bring home 200 pounds
of healthy potting soil
and 50 flowerpots,
enough to propagate
the cuttings of all the colorful
    violets
she was going to grow,
because she would need a lot
of flowers to give away
as interesting, thoughtful gifts

to newborn babies
and wedding gifts
to brides and grooms,
cheery solace for sick rooms
of those in her church
who fell ill.
She was under medical orders
to send a gift of flowers
for all the celebrations
and occasions
of everyone in her church.
When the church bazaar came
    around,
she was to send a score of
    violets
for the sale.
Now, you can imagine
how this changed her life,
can you not?
Erickson gave the gift of
    giving
as a permanent prescription
for her lonely sadness.
He knew that caring and
    self-care
are the same,
and understood how friendly
    and social
bodies want to be.

CHAINS AND FENCES

A Trance About Altruism and Connectedness

As you relax,
the mind becomes
an open field,
where wildflowers drift
in the breeze,
and birds of curiosity
settle from time to time
to contemplate the meaning
of my words,
then fly away again,
leaving you in quiet solitude,
peaceful wanderer,
moving toward a fluid horizon,
because when you experience
the inner peace of trance,
the unconscious mind may
turn to peaceful thoughts,
suddenly free
of ice-cold wars,
tearing down walls,
breaking boundaries
once covered with guns
and building bridges
        everywhere
to link the world together
in common aims
and shared responsibilities,
connecting each to the other,
links in a chain
that replace bricks and stone
with the chain link fences
of playgrounds and backstops,
where teams are formed,
and games are played,
and children of all ages
push each other
on swings,
and offer each other
assistance after the fall,
or share their lunches
just for the fun of it,
and the Dalai Lama
speaks of a "zone of peace"
at the roof of the world,
Tibet,
where inner peace,
and harmony,
sing the chants of
the pleasure
of riding high together,
of taking another
along for the thrill,
and joining with the doves,
that coo a song of love,
because caring for the children
in each of us is easy,
when the game begins
with new rules
in this new age
and we enjoy the warmth
of doing something,
of giving something,
to another,
where the door can open

in that fence
between us and the other,
and let them in
while it lets us out,
into the warm sun
of the field
of flowers

where the mind drifts
back upwards,
and becomes awakened
to the pleasures,
the treasures
waiting there.

8

NATURAL PLEASURES

Pleasure is vital to our well-being and our five senses are an accessible resource of various heady and healthy pleasures. This chapter provides scripts for the wholesome task of mining the senses for all they can bring to our lives.

While the notion that pleasure is good for us may seem obvious, Ornstein and Sobel (1989) note, "Many of us are phobic about having fun" (p. 13). They trace this sentiment to our puritanical mores and point to current medical and mental health biases against the pursuit of pleasure. They note that, generally speaking, our medical and psychological "treatments" tend to be subtractive and controlling in nature. Presumably, good mental health is obtained through careful monitoring for signs of trouble and rigid control over our behavior. Thus therapists may prescribe the elimination of "negative self-talk" for the depressed or the removal of "food cues" for the obese, and suggest that constant vigilance is necessary to prevent a relapse into workaholism, foodaholism, alcoholism, codependency, sexual addiction, and so on. Medicine and psychology are better at telling us what to avoid than at providing suggestions for health-giving pursuits. Yet there are abundant sensual and mental pleasures that promote health and increased longevity (cf. Ornstein & Sobel, 1989).

The fragrance of peaches reduces pain and the smell of spiced apples lessens stress (Brody, 1986). Beautiful music played during surgery lowers a patient's anesthesia requirements (Bonny & McCarron, 1984). Carbohydrates relax us and may elevate our mood (Wurtman, 1986). Massage is an effective treatment for anxiety and comforting touch slows a racing heart (McKechnie, Wilson, Watson, & Scott, 1983). Sex, sunsets, chocolate, learning, gardening, the things that give us pleasure, also strengthen the immune system, fill us with hope, and give our lives meaning (cf. Ornstein & Sobel, 1989).

Milton Erickson understood the healing value of pleasure. He used magic tricks, word games, and practical jokes to engage attention and to amuse (cf. Rosen, 1982). He even encouraged a sexually rigid husband to give pet names to his spouse's breasts (Haley, 1985). His interventions also often got his clients intimately involved with their senses. He once sent a lonesome, phobic man into the Arizona desert with the instruction to walk "until you find a reason for being glad you went down there" (Erickson, in Haley, 1985, Vol. I, p. 116). The man returned to Erickson to describe with wonder the beauty of a saguaro cactus and a blooming palo verde he had seen. Erickson also taught a man being fed through a tube how to enjoy a good burp and a paraplegic woman how to have orgasms in her earlobes (Haley, 1985).

As clinicians, we have become intent on prescribing pleasures for our clients. For most, this is simply a question of honing and intensifying skills clients already have. For others, it involves the more difficult issue of overcoming rigid prohibitions and learning to allow new experiences into awareness. Our scripts are "enjoyment maps"—happiness and health are the final destinations.

SWADDLING CLOTHES

A Trance to Enhance the Enjoyment of the Sense of Touch

It can be reassuring to notice
the feeling of the chair
as it supports your body,
the feeling of the muscles
at the back of the neck
as you continue to
relax
and my voice
can become a massage
of words,
gently easing all tension
in the arms,
in the legs,
in the shoulders,
and you might allow my words
to touch you more deeply or
they may simply glide over
    you,
like soothing water,
as you drift down more
    completely,
reflecting on the power of
    touch
to heal and to please,
to tease and to comfort.
In olden times
we swaddled newborn babies,
wrapping them snugly
in bands of white cloth,
so these babies could relax,
and sleep more deeply,
for the cuddling feeling
of their swaddling clothes.

We are just beginning
to learn the importance
of touch,
and the senselessness
of touch deprivation.
In hospitals across the country
the smallest of babies rest
while gentle, unrelenting touch
is given to them
and moves their legs,
their arms, in rhythmic
    fashion,
the cushioning of back and hips
with firm, warm hands
will send a massage to the
    brain,
"Grow!"
"Be well!"
"Respond now!"
it says,
and babies touched like this
begin to come alive,
are more in touch
with their surroundings,
and their moods are calmer,
more balanced.
"He was held back," we say.
She felt for the things
she imagined, but did not do.
We lose touch with our old
    friends,
and kindness touches us
more than we can express.

We are surrounded
by metaphors of touch,
encircled by a sensitive
and feeling skin,
which responds to warmth,
to breezes,
which reaches out
to kitten fur,
and iris petals,
and knows
sandpaper from silk.
We lift a hand in friendship,
high-five,
and caress a loved one.
Sometimes we stand
too close to the fire,
and know this immediately.
The vocabulary of feeling
is deeply textured,

feeling our way
through the dark,
at times,
searching for the switch we
    need
to bathe the room in light,
and prop ourselves up
on fluffy pillows,
wrap the favorite afghan
around us,
feel the steaming cup
between our fingers,
and slide down
like fingers on a trombone,
slide into
those deep notes of relaxation,
wrapped in our own
swaddling clothes,
safe and warm.

VISIONS

A Trance for Visual Pleasures

A child
in Catholic school
learns of the visible
and the invisible,
angels with rhyming names,
cherubim and seraphim,
could not be seen
by human eyes,
were spirits,
who wrestled with the sainted,
or arrived at your door
when you least expected them,

asking for kindnesses,
and sang in the sky
when God did something
especially wondrous,
and the holiest of men and
    women
had visions,
of God, of angels,
who would tell them secrets
about the substance of heaven,
and about the fate of the earth.
And the schoolchildren

wanted to have visions too,
wanted to be good enough
to see the angels,
or even to come face-to-face
with God.
Later,
in the gleaming armor
of the world,
angels and visions are
         forgotten.
"Seeing is believing," we say,
but we seldom see
and really don't believe,
for if we did,
we would recognize the visions
as they come knocking,
a perfect baby's head,
the bits of gold fleck
in a loved one's eyes,
the shimmer of the Texas hills,
after acres of flat and low,
the light of autumn,
all are visions that
we tend to overlook,
constricted by the shapes
of everyday life,
like a horse with blinders,
who sees nothing
but what is in our path.
I have a friend
who calls out "Hawk!"
during driving conversations,
not wanting me to miss
a chance to see the grace and
         beauty

of this bird in flight,
and even people blind from
         birth
see shades of light
in their night,
like Helen Keller,
who longed
most of all
for "three days to see,"
and detailed all the sights
she would fill herself full of
if only she could.
And I wonder what sights
you cherish most,
what shapes and shadows,
colors and silhouettes,
you would choose to see
if given just three days to
         see?
Remembering,
you have a lifetime
of visions to behold,
a life of light so precious
to the body's moods and
         rhythms,
the mind a shining surface,
reflecting,
the mind a creviced surface,
scattering,
our everyday visions
of fire's pale gold,
sunsets and purple skies,
and everyday visions
of saints
and angels.

CHRISTMAS CANDY

A Trance to Enhance the Enjoyment of Tastes

Four days into January,
the ornaments are packed
      away,
and only the eccentric
      neighbors
will keep the outdoor lights
twinkling in the front yard
'til Valentine's Day,
so we can pause and wonder
what to do
with the remaining
Christmas candy,
the kind from your childhood,
hard candy,
shaped like pieces of ribbon,
bright colors, circles of
      raspberry,
with white centers,
and none of it ever tasted
the way you might imagine,
which, of course,
can also be said
of Christmas itself.
Take a yellow candy,
certain to be lemon,
tastes of licorice instead,
and green lime of cinnamon,
the cherry reds turn out to
      be
vanilla,
and some are indecipherable,
sort of ginger,

sort of honey,
the tastes of Christmas,
the tastes of childhood,
mysterious and homey.
Food and holidays,
flavors juggle in the mind,
beads of moisture form
around an icy glass
of lemonade on the Fourth of
      July,
and the sweet and sour of it
tastes delicious.
Chocolate is an emotional food,
in heart-shaped boxes,
for the ones we love
the most,
creamy and luscious, they melt
irresistibly on the tongue,
and linger, like love,
long after the first heady taste
has disappeared.
Montezuma drank an extra cup
of chocolate, cocoa,
to fortify himself,
and his ardor,
before he spent an evening
in his harem.
And Easter is a feast,
a salty ham,
deviled eggs,
lamb with mint sauce,
a holy feast of breaking bread,

and drinking sacred wine,
food for redemption
and food for freedom,
like Passover food,
we eat to commemorate
and to remind us.
Whole fortunes of Europe,
nations, have been built
on the desire for spice alone,
ships launched
to Madagascar, Java,
        Indonesia,
in search of vanilla and pepper,
cinnamon and cloves,
as rich as jewels,
and pineapple still reminds us
of tropical breezes,
spices as predictable as
        timetables,
as they flood us with memories

and fill us with contentment.
Strings of tied garlic
and peppers
hang in modern kitchens . . .
evoking taste nostalgia
and drawing the mind
toward the simple pleasures
        of
taste and smell,
where we are still surprised
by new tastes
like children reaching
        deep
into their stockings
for still another new delight,
and we revel in the comfort
of the old familiar taste
that soothes us,
like the holiday taste
of Christmas candy.

AROMA THERAPY

A Trance to Enhance the Enjoyment of Smells

Memory and smell
waft, woven in the mind,
each of us carrying our own
pack of scent-laden
rememberings.
My grandmother always wore
lily-of-the-valley perfume,
and I can't help but wonder,
as your mind wanders,
what particular scents
are meaningful events

for you?
The musty attic,
reminiscent,
baking bread and cookies,
or the scents of pineapple
and coconut,
triumphantly tropical,
rush like salty waves
on the mind's shores.
So unexpectedly,
the smell of papier-mâché

brings back our child efforts
to build castles, animals, and
    moats,
and freshly mowed grass
    brings
summer evenings exploding
gently in our memory,
a fireworks of fragrance,
let off in
a field of dreams.
Smell is the basic sense
and the most direct,
five million cells will fire
the impulse of smell
toward the target of the mind
and heart,
straight as an arrow,
past the reasoning brain,
to rest
smoldering in our primitive
    mind,
seat of emotion,
place of ancient longings,
desires,
and wisdom.
Smell is the language
of our ancestors,
and yet it needs no interpreter,
though the shape of smell
will mold itself
to changing times
and changing places.
On my mother's dresser
are many small bottles,
delicate, long-stemmed vials,
of perfume,
fragrance for the Western
    warrior,
while Masai women dress their
    hair
with dung,
a sharp, staccato odor,
considered beautiful
and full of lust.
In the temples of Egypt
aromatic medicine emerged,
the healing power of fragrance
was well known
and well respected
throughout the ancient world,
frankincense and myrrh
were valuable as gold,
as unguents for pregnancy
and birth.
Cinnamon, both stimulant and
    antiseptic,
and jasmine, deep, sweet,
    warming,
a cure for lethargy,
healing smells forgotten,
then resurrected again
during the Renaissance,
so Marco Polo sailed the world
in search of exotic spices
and their perfumes,
and whales we sought
for ambergris
and animals for musk,
and today we rediscover
the ancient restorations,
another renaissance
where we are surprised to find
that the smell of spiced apples
lowers blood pressure
and makes the anxious person
calm,

and lavender speeds
    metabolism
and a lover's smell
heighten's fertility,
as science reinvents
the age-old knowing

of our complex evolution,
of the power of aroma
to heal,
and comfort,
and distill
memories.

UNCHAINED MELODIES

A Trance to Enhance the Enjoyment of Sounds

Sounds may bubble
in the background,
as you drift down
into your own mind,
your special place
of calm relaxation,
like summer twilight,
lying on the shore
and listening
to the shrill cries of frogs,
and the splashes of the
gray wading birds,
the hum of insects
and motors slowing
as they enter
the "No Wake" zone,
while children laugh
in the background
and the mind moves quietly,
like fish following bait
through still waters,
and a fisherman sighs,
knowing he's been
played another prank.
Outer space is silent,

but here on earth
we live within a Milky Way
of sounds,
though we have learned
to tune out much
of what we hear.
There is a store
in Austin, Texas,
called "Out of Africa,"
which deals in African music
and artifacts,
and the room is filled
with music
from South Africa and Kenya,
from Ethiopia and Sierra
    Leone,
vibrant choruses of drums,
    voices
ringing like bells,
and the owner is waiting,
ready to explain
the myriad of music
to his customers.
Yet I have never seen anyone
buy any music there.

Customers ask,
"Do you have the music
from the movie *Out of Africa?*"
and leave, disappointed,
because he does not.
They don't even hear
the real African music
resonating throughout the
    room,
and I can't help but wonder
what might happen if
we are able to set ourselves
    free
from our sound cocoons,
and really hear,
eavesdrop on the music
of many different worlds,
really hear the voices of
our loved ones,
the songs of birds,
and water splashing in a
    fountain,
hear the sounds bouncing

off our bodies,
know the echoes of our own
    heart,
like the scientists who have
    translated
the beating heart
into musical notes
and discovered that everyone
    plays
their own special heart-song.
Does one person's heart
play a violin,
another a trumpet?
And what of yours,
what does it play now?
Each of us carries
exquisite sounds
within ourselves,
and our music may blend
with all the sounds
of the universe,
the music
of the spheres.

BEACHES

A Trance for Synesthesia

Did you know
that if you evoke
the relaxation response
while running,
you go faster,
with less effort,
which is just a good way of
    saying

that you really can relax,
here, now,
and know you'll soon get to
where you want to go.
And where you want to go
is more than one place,
a mingling of sensual
    destinations

is there for you,
because something called
    synesthesia
is built into our senses,
though we often overlook it,
(or undersmell it),
trained as we are
to keep our experiences
in separate boxes and
    compartments,
taking them out one at a time.
For now I would like to invite
    you
to have the luxury of
spilling all the boxes out at
    once,
hearing the sounds of each
    color
you see in your mind's eye,
and smelling sunlight
on the skin.
A great place for this
is on the beach . . .
so let's travel there.
Everyone is happy at the
    beach,
usually,
umbrella colors, air tastes yel-
    low salt,
and neon bathing suits
float by,
five elderly women holding
    hands
and screaming with joy
as they wade deeper
into icy water,
hot bodies, cold surf blending
    into

singular sensations.
The design of beach chairs
seems so perfect,
body close to the ground,
toes buried in the sand,
turning the radios, laughter,
children's voices,
into a gentle roar
of soothing sound
that sparkles in the mind
and tingles the toes,
white sand sounds
and french fries,
salt and sugar tastes
curling like waves
around the ankles,
the knees, the shoulders,
banana-coconut oils
sliding down the back
of your arms
and the back
of your throat,
smooth, slippery smells,
fruity tastes,
watching the little girl
do somersaults.
Before each one she asks,
"Do you want to see?"
Mother always answers Yes
and watches her
through rose-colored glasses,
She's turning in the air—a
    kite—
a white sail, a white cap,
a white hot whiff
of clams
drifts and the girl drifts,
motionless,

suspended
in white light,
salt,
sea,

sand,
bright,
colors all
together.

9

HEALTHY SUCCESSES

Success in any endeavor depends on a variety of factors, some controllable and some not. At a minimum, however, success seems to require a genuine desire to excel, to accomplish a goal. Even the most gifted will fail if they do not pursue success with an intense passion. This became obvious to A.L. Samuel (1959) as he worked to perfect the first computerized checkers player. Although his machine could compute all possible outcomes of a given move, initially it was just a mediocre player. It made only "safe" moves that prevented it from losing, which meant that most games ended in a draw. Not until Samuel added a program that instructed the machine to play to win was it able to defeat champion players. On a more human scale, Atkinson and Feather (1966) determined that a high need to achieve is a prerequisite to outstanding performance in all aspects of life, whereas its opposite, an ongoing effort to avoid failure, rarely leads to more than mediocrity.

Maddi and Kosaba (1984) also found that a genuine desire to succeed (i.e., a high degree of *commitment* to the task) is related to success, but these authors were more impressed by the fact that such an attitude has the additional benefit of making the task less stressful. Some people pay a high price physically and psychologically to succeed and some do not. Those who maintain a high degree of commitment to their goals experience fewer effects of stress in their work, perhaps because they enjoy it more (cf. Csikszentmihalyi, 1990).

Commitment is one of the primary ingredients in the broader cognitive schema Maddi and Kosaba call *psychological hardiness,* a collection of attitudes that minimize levels of stress on the road to success. The other two ingredients are a sense of personal *control* over external events (efficacy) and a belief that the ongoing changes in life represent a continuous *challenge* for further development (optimism). These two factors are usually considered to be components of optimism and were dealt with directly in Chapter 6. Thus the following scripts deal primarily with the issue of commitment, that is, the motivation to achieve or excel versus the desire to avoid failure.

STAR BRIGHT

A Trance to Foster the Ingredients of Success

Waiting now,
silently wondering,
as you relax,
whatever happened to that
    child
who used to wish upon a star,
who wanted something so
    badly
and genuinely believed
it could come true,
who listened to the stories
about the little engine that
    could,
and would feel the happy
    ending,
knowing it can,
and you can too,
and finding that recognition,
that every moment
is another chance
to use,
to get there,
to get where you want to be,
because there was this boy
who used to be a star,
he excelled at everything,
sports and school and friends,
until that day
he made a mistake,
and the other team won,
and he was teased
and vowed right there
never to do that again,

so he retreated into safety,
not doing anything risky,
not taking any chances,
always afraid
that there was a mistake
to be made,
always aware
that things could go wrong,
and he started playing lousy,
and felt bad too,
so bad he sought help,
something to undo,
and so he came in for therapy
and just listened to a story
about the first attempts
to program a computer
to play checkers,
and how it could not win
because it was trying not to
    lose,
and needed to be told
to make each move to win,
to always press the advantage,
to find a winning move,
and never to doubt for a minute
that it could succeed,
because it had the ability,
it just needed to use it well,
to know it could,
to enjoy that feeling
of knowing what to do,
because you know
where you want to go

and how to get there,
and you can too,
as you remember
that feeling,
the pleasure of knowing
each moment is an opportunity,
a chance given to you,
to do what you **can** do,
and to enjoy doing it too,
to want to do
what you can do
to make it to the top,
with that little star inside
granting your every wish,
a source of energy and
    warmth,
a source of guidance,
and the secure knowledge
that all things come
to those who cannot not do
    it,
to those who are using
everything they are
to go as high and far
as they wish,
upon that star.

JUST DO IT

A Trance for the Desire to Succeed

It would be fine
if all there was to it
was to just do it,
and that would do it,
but starting to do
is sometimes as hard,
especially when
you are afraid to screw it
up, or are not sure
that you can,
or even want to do
what you want to do,
and so you begin
to think, now,
about how the little engine
could and did,
and how it feels
to feel that fire burning,
that passion hot inside,
that fuels the cells
in the mind,
where all that energy
is locked up,
held back, kept in,
like the child
on that boring weekend,
who felt so cooped up inside
that he was pacing and sighing,
wanting someone to take him
someplace, anyplace,
where he could **do something,**
so they took him to the lake
where there are huge mounds
of rocks,
and he threw and threw
as far as he could,
as big as he could hold,
just to be doing something

challenging,
something that made him
feel better,
because doing that
was better than nothing,
like a racehorse colt,
tied in the barn,
full of energy
waiting for spring,
dancing and prancing in place,
wanting to spring out
of that place,
feeling the pent-up
energy,
the driving desire to do,
to have the thrill
of the challenge
do it better than before,
to do more and more,
to turn that self free,
to let it do whatever
it wants to do,
to succeed at anything
is worth doing.

And you can succeed at
    anything
you decide you want to do,
because there are always
ways of letting that energy
    out,
letting it burn a path
straight to that goal,
no goalies in the way,
just opportunities
at every turn,
as you take your turn,
and feel that yearning
desire to do,
to just do
it
now,
just as you
begin to drift up, now,
and return reeling
with that feeling,
that you can
and want to, too.

CARRY ON

A Trance to Stimulate the Desire to Succeed

The goal of relaxation,
of restful tranced awareness,
is a very different goal
from the goal of following
your dreams,
Lof doing those things
that you really want to do,
because you wait for a trance,

you wait in a trance,
and someone waits on you,
feeding you what you need
or want,
but did not give yourself,
waking later on
knowing what you're going
to do,

following your bliss,
not sitting there,
letting it take you
to the top,
because it does not matter
what anyone does,
as long as they do it,
like the man who loved trains,
so he built model railroads
as a hobby,
until one day this interest,
this play,
became what he did
for a living,
just like the ballplayer,
and the thinker,
doing what they did best,
doing what they enjoyed,
and enjoying doing it best
because that is what they do,
or the golfer, or the inventor,
the writer and the diver,
the driver and the talker,
doing what they do,
because even a loser
can win at something,
and what that something is
only that person knows
for sure,
finding the courage
to admit it
and carry on with it,
which is what made Mary
determined to take it easy,
and to cook for a living,
because she was lazy
and just wanted to do
what she enjoyed most,

what was fun, not work,
so she went to school,
first in New York,
then in Paris,
and ended up graduating
first in her class,
which was fun,
becoming a first-class chef,
with offers from the finest
restaurants in the world,
when all she wanted to do
was to take it easy
and enjoy herself,
following her bliss,
and she did
and does now too,
thinking she is the luckiest
person in the world,
getting a chance to do
exactly what she wants to do,
and being able to do it so well
that they pay her to do it
        too,
and so can you,
do it, too,
because it all
belongs to you
for you to free yourself
to do it now,
and you know how
to enjoy the value
of those efforts
that amount to play
when you do what you
want to do,
and try to let
anyone stop you,
including you,

as you begin to feel
the unconscious decide
to take you there,
even as it takes you
back here now,

awareness,
back to the wakeful
where the mind opens
as the eyes open
as well.

10

PEAK MENTAL AND PHYSICAL PERFORMANCE

Continued success and satisfaction in any endeavor rest on a foundation of positive mental sets, innate talents, and thorough preparation. These basic ingredients make reaching the top possible, and, just as important, they also generate a sense of well-being along the way. However, to bring all of these ingredients together and use them to produce peak performance in a specific setting, the individual must be able to pay attention in the right way to the right things at that particular moment. A lapse in concentration or a momentary distraction can produce errors in judgment and performance in even the most competent person. Those who excel in academic, sports, or business activities are those who manage their attention effectively.

The effective management of attention for peak performance begins with the ability to focus attention in an unwavering manner—that is, the ability to concentrate on what you are doing. If you are trying to hit a baseball, you must pay attention to the ball and not to your own thoughts or to an itch in your foot. On the other hand, if you are trying to solve a complex problem, you must attend to your thoughts, not to baseballs. Concentration enhances learning (Underwood, 1976), problem solving and creativity (Vernon, 1970), memory (Klatzky, 1984), and physical performance (Keele, 1973).

It must be emphasized that competent concentration involves a detached, observant state of stable awareness, a state referred to by Gallwey (1974) as "unfreakability" and "relaxed concentration." Critical mental sets and conscious concerns must be suspended to accomplish full concentration. A nonjudgmental state of mind allows the individual to observe events without anxiety or interference. It is the state of mind necessary to acquire new information or skills. Lozanov (1978), for example, used music to create a condition of absorbed but noncritical attention to maximize the rapid learning of a foreign language. He called this state of mind "concert pseudopassiveness." Gilligan (1987) used the term "controlled spontaneity" to describe the liberating absorption underlying exceptional performances of professional musicians, basketball players, innovative thinkers, and master therapists.

Whatever this state is called, becoming absorbed in this manner has impressive consequences. The mind of the archer rides the arrow to the bull's-eye; the quarterback turns his back, knowing that the pass is perfect and the ball will be caught; the musician becomes lost in the beauty of her or his own playing; and the therapist knows things about the client before there is any obvious evidence for the insight. Bill Russell of the Boston Celtics says that such experiences make him feel "free and high as a skyhawk" (Russell, 1979). When anyone "goes with the flow" in this manner, it enables the mind/body to move and react with the sense of effortless grace and perfection associated with peak performances. Because it is so similar to a hypnotic trance, almost any induction approach can be used to teach this state. The first script presented below, however, is specifically constructed to describe and instill the ability for observant, absorbed concentration.

The second step in the development of attention management for peak performance involves the ability to broaden or narrow the focus of absorbed attention in response to the demands of the situation. Different types of activities require a different breadth of focus of attention. For example, a narrow focus of attention is necessary for individual efforts, such as those of a target shooter, a pool player, or a gymnast (Maxeiner, 1987), but a broad or open focus is required for team sports such as soccer, hockey, and football (Nettleton, 1986). The second script in this chapter offers instructions for opening and closing the focus of attention.

Finally, some activities demand that attention be directed internally toward specific thoughts or sensations, and other activities require attention to be directed externally. For example, Wrisberg and Pein (1990) report that experienced long-distance runners tend to focus their attention on external events (music, scenery), whereas inexperienced runners tend to focus on painful internal bodily sensations. Similarly, Padgett and Hill (1989) indicate that performance in endurance events, such as long-distance running, increases when athletes focus attention externally. Mahoney (1991) complicates the picture a bit by noting that the truly "elite" marathon runners do not focus externally but focus instead on their internal physical sensations. They simply do not label these feelings as pain. Hence in endurance activities either attention should be focused externally or the performer must be able to attend to bodily sensations in a detached way, not viewing them as painful. Most intellectual and creative activities also involve an internal focus, though some pursuits, such as speed reading and painting, may require an external orientation. In each instance, a nonevaluative state of mind is preferable and more productive. The final script in this chapter gives clients a chance to master the ability to shift a noncritical focus of attention either internally or externally.

SESAME STREET

A Trance for Enhanced Concentration

Now,
you already know
that in everything you do,
you always do much better
if you pay attention,
if you keep your minds,
your conscious mind
and your unconscious mind,
on what you are doing,
if you become absorbed,
completely lost,
undistracted
from that one thing,
that one job,
that one book,
that one person,
absolutely lost
in whatever you are doing.
And that state of mind
is so easy to experience,
so easy to enter,
when we allow it to occur.
Even a small child
does it so easily
when there is something
of great interest,
something fascinating,
something important to
    observe,
like watching that program on
    TV,
"Sesame Street,"
where animals speak
and sing and dance
and teach how to read,
about letters
and numbers,
counting apples and oranges,
going places, doing things,
things that fascinated little
    Daniel
and held him glued to the
    screen,
captivated by the learnings,
entranced by the words,
lost in the images,
amused by the songs,
totally absorbed,
totally interested
in watching and hearing,
in learning and doing,
engaged by the puppets
speaking directly to him,
so interested in them
that nothing else mattered,
nothing else existed,
not even his mother calling,
or his brother playing,
or his hunger
even entered his mind
as he watched
from 7 to 9.
And those things
that you want to do,

each thing that you do,
has something in it to find,
something to create,
that absorbs you too,
and lets you know
that that is all
you want to do,
all you want to know
for a while,
because
there is something there,
something for you,
or something about
someone you know,
something you know
you need to know,
and now that you know
the mind gets stuck,
like special glue,
fastened right there
on that,
the mind boiled down,
concentrated
in one place
on one thing,
focused,
with great intensity,
an intense feeling,
the fascination,
with concentration,
the anticipation
that now you can,
now you do,
focus your attention,
direct it right there then,
right on what you want to,
on what you need to,
whenever you want,

feeling the mind absorbed by
    it,
a magnetic pull,
attracting attention to it,
just turning on a switch,
and things click in
and the mind goes there,
only there,
only aware,
no distracting thoughts
or sights or sounds,
just being aware,
soaking it all up,
absorbing all there is,
because nothing else matters,
for a time,
nothing else exists,
for a time,
lost in that moment
in time,
anytime you wish,
an ability to allow
your unconscious mind
to find that thought,
to find that feeling
that pulls you right into it,
that lets you know
to pay close attention to it,
and you can do it now,
feeling that feeling,
absorbed in that moment,
and when you know
that you do know how,
and can do it now,
you can drift back up
to the surface
of wakeful awareness,
drifting back

and waking up now.
That's right,
wide awake,
but able to return

to that absorption
anytime you want to,
anytime you need to.
That's right.

TRAVELOGUES

Trance Training for Open and Closed Focus of Attention

Now that you know
how to allow
the mind to sit still,
to relax and focus,
you can take a trip,
a small journey,
where you can learn
something new,
another thing
that you can do,
to master the mind
and use it more fully,
a short vacation,
the kind you see
in travelogues,
movies for the mind,
where you sit and relax,
the lights go dim,
the movie begins
about another time,
another place,
a future time and place,
where the picture starts
with an image of a flower,
focused up close
on just that flower,
its deep color,

the petals and pollen,
so close you can touch it,
and just the sound of buzzing
as a bee lands in the middle,
but then the camera pulls back,
the focus broadens,
other things come into view,
the surrounding flowers,
the hillside,
the city all around,
with the sounds of traffic,
horns and rushing tires,
the noise of people,
laughter and surprise,
a flower in a garden,
on a hill,
in a city,
a city that surrounds
on all sides,
then back we go
to that flower,
the camera narrows our view
and slowly moves back to
that flower,
all alone,
waving in the breeze,
the colors,

a drop of dew,
the bee returns
and the buzz does too,
a narrow view,
a tight view,
like opening and closing
the mind,
closing in on one thing,
opening out to everything,
focusing on this thing,
aware of all those things,
and you can feel it now,
the camera of the mind,
that zooms in tight, at times,
a close-up view of a hand,
    perhaps,
or even a finger,
or the sensations
under a fingernail,
tightening that focus,
looking at that one thing,
aware of narrowing down,
aware that you can be aware
of the tiniest of feelings
    there,
a pinpoint feeling,
so small,
and yet
the mind can open
as well,
spreading out awareness
to cover the entire body,
aware of the body resting
    there,
sensations from everywhere,
able to notice those thoughts
    too,
and those sounds

and the images sent by the
    eyes,
then closing back down,
the small flowering sensation,
that tiny place on a hand,
or a finger,
closing in to notice one
    thing,
then opening right out,
expanding that scene,
the whole body returns,
open again to it all,
taking it all in,
everything,
but able to go
back in again,
back in to a toe, perhaps,
some tiny patch of skin,
examining it in detail,
then back out again,
opening and closing,
exercising that ability,
learning to move out and in,
the way that cameraman did
in that film,
a flower in a city,
narrow view
blocks all else out,
but you can move out
to take it all in,
using that ability,
opening out,
closing in,
in whatever way
is right for you
in every situation,
using that ability
almost automatically,

and able to enjoy the view,
wide or narrow,
it all belongs to you,
even as you drift up now,
opening that view even more,
the floor, the lights,
the chair,
learning with returning,

learning as you wake up
now,
wide awake,
widening the mind,
narrowing the mind,
back and forth
even as you are wide awake,
now.

SCREEN DOORS

Trance Training for Internal and External Focus of Attention

On a quiet summer day
you can relax,
stay inside
or go out,
stay in,
where it is dark and cool,
or go out,
where it is bright and warm,
or go out,
then come back inside,
just by going through
a door,
a screen door, perhaps,
that you can see through,
seeing the shady trees,
feeling the soft warm breeze,
knowing you can go out,
and once out you can go back
    in,
while the mind drifts out,
aware of the sounds out here,
out in this room,
hearing the noises
even before

you open your eyes, now,
staying in a trance,
just going outside
to explore,
just opening that door,
opening the eyes,
that's right,
looking out,
reaching out
with eyes and ears,
feeling the texture
of the things you see,
touching the colors
with your eyes
out there,
or do those colors
touch you?
Aware of out there,
the room and lights,
the sounds and things
outside that door,
then going back in,
eyes still open,
mind traveling in,

back through that door,
back in to thoughts,
the sensations,
that inner world
inside that door,
able to see out
but feeling inside,
exploring the images
that drift through the mind,
watching the sensations
dancing about
in a hand or an arm,
or somewhere inside,
just watching what happens
in there,
then going back out,
coming back out here,
out into this room,
the other side of the screen,
out into the light,
out into the sounds,
looking around,
the outside world
reveals itself to you,
then back through that door,
back in to explore
inside that door,
inside the mind,
inside the body,
an inner awareness,
an inner recognition,
that you can move the mind
down into a foot or a leg,
up to a shoulder,
up to those thoughts,
the attic of the mind,
where things drift and float,

then back toward that door
    again
and out,
back outside here,
even aware
of the crispness of the air
as you return to this room,
the things in the room,
the sounds coming in,
just watching,
observing,
no need to do anything,
just noticing those things
as the mind discovers,
even more than before,
that you can be here,
and in a trance too,
and you can stay here
as that trance dissolves
and the mind returns
to wakeful alertness,
completely awake,
comfortably aware,
knowing,
more than before,
how to go through that door,
in or out
of trance,
anytime.
That's right,
wide awake now,
but go in . . .
back through that door,
back inside . . .
then come back out . . .
back out here . . .
before we stop, now.

11

MEDITATIVE STATES

Within the spiritual traditions of the East, there are many different forms of attention training or meditation (cf. Goleman, 1977; Hanson, 1973; Naranjo & Ornstein, 1971; Watts, 1957; White, 1974). Each form of meditation serves at least two purposes. One is the development of sophisticated attention management skills and the other is the use of these new skills to create transformational experiences that provide alternative, mystical perspectives on oneself and reality. The hypnosis scripts presented here teach the attention management skills associated with three different types of Eastern meditation: *samatha*, *vipassana*, and *sunyata*. The scripts in the following chapter are designed to stimulate experiences similar to the altered states of consciousness or enlightenment sought by those who engage in regular practice of these forms of attention management.

Obviously, meditation can be practiced and mastered without using hypnosis. However, a hypnotic trance offers a comfortable introduction to the meditative experience because entry into a hypnotic trance relies on modifications in attention that are comparable to those involved in meditation (Davidson & Goleman, 1977).

A light trance is appropriate for these meditative hypnosis sessions because a client needs to be consciously aware of the instructions and able to carry them out intentionally later on. A deep, dissociative trance would make this difficult. The light trance state facilitates the required steady focus of attention and offers a calm, comfortable climate in which to practice and get used to the meditative experience.

These meditative trance experiences are most suitable for individuals who are basically stable and interested in personal growth. The experience of meditative trance can be disconcerting for those who are not yet ready to alter their reality (Epstein, 1990) and may be of little use to those who are stuck in depressive or anxiety-producing cognitive schemas (Tart & Deikman, 1991).

Participants should be told that they may experience various unusual perceptions, sensations, or emotions while they are meditating and that this is perfectly normal. This also applies to unusual physical movements, such as minor twitches or sudden small spasms in an arm, a leg, or a finger. The general rule of thumb seems to be that whatever happens is just fine as long as it is brief and has no long-term consequences. Participants should be instructed to notice such events quietly and then return to the meditative exercise.

THE MAGNIFYING GLASS

A Trance Session for Teaching Focused Meditation

This script offers guidelines for transforming hypnotic trance into the meditative state of *samatha*, or one-pointedness. The instructions offered in this script are similar to those employed by Benson (1975). In this meditative approach, our goal is the creation of a stable focus of attention that is directed exclusively, for an extended time, toward one particular thing, such as a sound, a mentally repeated word, or an image (Rahula, 1959). The meditator sits absolutely still and directs his or her attention to a pinpoint focus on the object of meditation. Although similar to a state of concentration, attention during this form of meditation is absorbed by one specific stimulus rather than a general topic or activity.

Obviously, participants should be told the purpose of this trance experience beforehand. A brief discussion of the potential benefits of this form of meditation also is appropriate. Such a discussion might include a summary of the findings of Wallace and Benson (1972), who reported significant reductions in blood lactate levels, respiratory rate, oxygen consumption, and other measures of physiological activation or stress. Reference to the long-term cognitive, emotional, and perceptual benefits described by authors such as Benson (1975) and Shapiro (1980) also is in order. Following the trance training session, participants are given a chance to discuss the experience and to ask questions.

Once the participant has used the trance experience successfully to enter this meditative state, the meditative exercise should be repeated twice a day, once in the morning and once in the late afternoon or early evening. Each session should take place prior to meals and should last 10 to 20 minutes. Instruct your client to sit in a comfortable position and repeat the same meditation process practiced in your office during hypnotic trance. We have not experienced any adverse reactions to this meditative procedure.

Benson (1975), however, cautions against excessive meditation (i.e., several hours a day).

You can sit there,
with your eyes closed,
and continue to relax
as you listen to me,
and follow along,
quite carefully,
paying attention,
waiting
for me to tell you
exactly what to do
to learn how
to tame the mind,
to fence it in
and to calm it down
to one thing,
because the mind
flies about
at the speed of light,
filling every corner
of the room,
and we need to know
exactly how
to focus it in,
to slow it down,
to concentrate it
in one spot,
the mind like a lens,
looking at just one thing.
So concentrate now
and examine this idea,
the same way
you might examine
one tiny speck
with a magnifying glass,
a clear glass shape

that focuses attention
on that one thing
as you examine it,
every single detail.
And that one thing
that I want you to examine,
that one thing to do
as you continue to relax
and let the mind focus in,
and look down within,
and repeat it over and over,
is one . . . , one . . . , one. . . .
Just one . . . , one . . . ,
        one . . . ,
repeating over and over,
getting softer and softer,
one . . . , one . . . , one . . . ,
so soft
you can barely hear it,
but it continues on,
one . . . , one . . . , one . . . ,
and all you need to do,
is to keep it there,
going on and on,
paying close attention to
        it,
always returning to it,
staying there with it,
repeating it over and over
until I tell you
it is time to stop,
that's right,
one . . . , one . . . , one. . . . ,
over and over,
and on and on,

one . . . , one . . . , one . . . ,
(Pause for about 10 minutes.)
That's right,
and very gently now
you can begin to stop
repeating that sound
and slowly return
your full attention
to the sound of my voice,
to the sounds in the room,
gradually returning

to normal, wakeful awareness,
letting the mind awaken
quite completely,
remembering how it feels
to meditate in that way,
always able to return there.
Resting quietly
for a moment or two,
and then
allowing the eyes
to open.

AN ELECTRIC RIVER

A Trance for Mindfulness

This script is designed to foster *vipassana*, or mindfulness, a condition wherein attention is directed toward a nonevaluative yet vigilant awareness of everything that is going on at the moment (cf. Davidson & Goleman, 1977; Kabat-Zinn, 1990). The mind is open to all events. Mindfulness meditation may be conducted during a special quiet period or incorporated as an ongoing state of mind throughout the course of an ordinary day. Our usual habit of attention is to keep track of what is going on around us by constantly shifting a narrow focus of attention from one thing to another. During mindfulness, the goal is to become broadly aware of everything at once. The focus of attention is opened wider and wider until it encompasses all thoughts, sensations, and perceptions.

And as you relax,
mind drifting along,
quite comfortable
just listening,
not doing anything
in particular,

you can begin to notice
that things begin to change,
as you become more
and more aware
of just how aware
you can be

of exactly where
an arm is positioned,
or a leg,
and what sounds you can
        hear.
Because the mind
becomes clear,
as you relax,
and things begin
to flow free,
the way a small mountain
        stream
begins at the top,
begins to flow down,
and gathers more and
        more
energy,
more and more clarity,
as it flows down further,
and the banks open wider,
like opening the dams
and letting it all flow
together,
the electric clarity,
the thoughts,
the sounds,
the sensations
from all around,
as the mind opens
each gate,
each window,
the curtains pull back,
the light shines in,
the energy flows through,
fills the mind
with a clear, full view
of everything
happening to you,

everything
happening around you,
as switches are turned on
in each room in the mind,
so the ears can hear,
the fingers can feel,
the mind can think,
so clearly and cleanly,
and it all flows together,
gathers energy together,
gets bigger and fuller
as the mind opens more,
letting more in,
more in at a time,
like a rainbow,
each in a row,
staying separate,
yet all there,
as you watch and feel
how they all are here,
all at once,
at the same time,
separate yet together,
the thoughts,
the sensations
from each part of the body,
inside and out,
all there at once,
all there together,
with the sounds and sights,
as you open your eyes now,
something new to add,
that's right,
adding those sights,
as your eyes stay still
but you see all around,
aware of how bright
as the light

fills the room,
but still fully aware
of everything
that was there
before.
Adding the images
to the sounds,
to the sensations
from all around,
adding them into
that ongoing flow,
that opening
of each channel
so it all flows in,
but it all stays apart,
like opening the mind
to two things at once,
then three and four
and more and more,
opening it up
to all at once,
to everything you see,
everywhere around,
everything you hear
around the room,
everything you think
about all those things,
all at once there,
an orchestral sound,

each separate,
yet there all together,
a symphony of life,
a full recognition
of each separate thing,
all at once,
all around.
And you can continue
to open your mind,
to split up awareness
to follow each thing,
to direct awareness
everywhere all at once,
to be aware
of everything there is
from moment to moment,
as it all
flows in,
fills the mind
that gets wider
and wider,
and fills with the wonder
of it all . . . ,
that's right,
brighter and fuller
as it all streams in,
aware of it all
for a while.
(*Pause for 10 minutes.*)

MOTHER, AM I?

A Trance for Complete Detachment

The final script in this chapter presents a form of meditation, *sunyata*, which involves a gradual letting go of any personal attachments to or identification with all personal thoughts, sensations, and perceptions until all sense of the self is eliminated from awareness altogether and only "nothingness" remains (cf. Naranjo & Ornstein, 1971; Novak, 1978). During this meditative process, attention gradually detaches from all aspects of the environment and from all aspects of the self. Everything that enters awareness is defined as "not me" and thus irrelevant. Eventually, the subject begins to lose a sense of identity and a sense of attachment to the ordinary flurry of thoughts and sensory impressions. Attention is all that remains, attention liberated from personal considerations and sociocultural expectations and beliefs. The person becomes aware only of awareness, and hence of nothing more than the essence of being (Novak, 1978). This "death of the self" is comparable to the state of mind sought by the samurai who wished to free themselves from all distractions caused by the fear of death (Herrigel, 1971) and is the precursor to the "cosmic consciousness" experience discussed in the following chapter.

Now,
as you rest here,
quietly aware,
we can play a game,
like a game from childhood,
only different,
because they used to
    say,
"Mother, may I?",
and now here today
we are going to say,

"Mother, am I?"
And each thing you
    find
in your mind,
each thought,
each sensation,
each awareness,
you can ask yourself
that question,
"Mother, am I this
    thought?"

"Am I this hand?"
"Am I this sensation?"
And each thing you notice,
each thing that crosses the
      mind,
you can simply say,
"No, that is not me."
And that is not either,
and neither is that,
because no matter what you
      see,
no matter what you hear,
no matter what you feel,
it is not **you,**
and even those thoughts
about what is
and what is not
will not be you either.
So go ahead now,
and play this game,
and notice how it feels
as you lighten your load,
letting go of one thing
and then another,
and then more parts later
      on,
not needing
to hold onto them,
because none of them
are you,
following that letting
      go
back to the beginning,
where there was you,
just you,
and you did not have
ears or hands,
did not have legs

or thoughts,
were just that tiny
      spark,
that sparkle of awareness,
that center of it all
that stays there
through it all
as you let go
of this and that
and everything
that is not you.
So go on through
letting go of you,
letting go of it all
right now,
because as you do
you move down into
the center of it all
that really is you,
all there is to you,
because this is not you,
and letting go
is not you too.
All there is to you
is the silent You you
      find
as you let it all
drift away,
it is not you,
so you let it go,
and then you find
what is *you.* . . .
(*Pause for at least five
      minutes.*)
And then,
gathering it all back
      up,
putting it back together

for now,
pulling yourself together,
though now you know
what is you
and what is not,
and you can return
to the center of you
playing that special
    game,
"Mother, am I?"
"No, I am not,"
whenever you want to,
though for now,
you may put you
back together.
Like putting on a costume,
a collection of things
that we call you,
just memories
and clothes,
just appearances
stuck to you
to cover the quiet,
the still calm
that is all there is to you,
which you put back on, now,

as you drift back up,
    now,
and remember who you
    are,
or who you are supposed to
    be,
being here right now,
the you
that is not you,
but they think it is,
so you can too,
if you wish,
for a while,
upon a star
that shines bright,
a light in the very middle,
that is really you,
even as you become
more and more the you
that you wanted to
before,
and returning now
to normal, wakeful awareness,
wide awake and back together,
back to you,
right **now.**

12

MYSTICAL STATES

The trance sessions presented in this chapter are designed to evoke approximations of intense alterations in consciousness referred to variously as peak experiences, *satori*, enlightenment, and cosmic consciousness. Many people experience mild, brief episodes of such states from time to time. You may have experienced a similar state of mind while making love, lost for a moment in waves of sensation. You may have felt it while playing a sport, awed by the unexpected perfection of a particular move. It may have arrived with the sunset colors in a quiet lake or you may have entered that state while simply painting a house, hiking a lovely mountain trail, or fixing breakfast on that one particularly beautiful morning. Some people have experienced this state at the very moment that they solved a difficult and complex mathematical problem. Peak experiences can happen during prayer, while looking at a great work of art, while playing chess, while working on a car, or while just sitting in an airport thinking about life.

During that moment of undistracted, unself-conscious awareness, our thoughts, perceptions, and sensations synthesize, and we feel completely at one with ourselves and the task at hand. We may feel an unself-conscious confidence in ourselves and our bodies. We can experience the inherent beauty and perfection of everything around us. We are filled with genuine tranquillity. At such times, we direct our attention toward our most nurturing and life-enhancing resources and, for that moment, we live our life to its fullest. These experiences usually are so transitory or disconnected from our ordinary life that when we "snap out of it," we find it difficult to describe or recreate. Once experienced, however, these moments are also difficult to forget. Sometimes they change our view of reality.

Accounts of such experiences are quite frequent and often are associated with outstanding insights or accomplishments. Maslow, of course, has provided numerous examples of peak experiences and has indicated that such events can change one's entire outlook on life (Maslow, 1975). Bucke (1900) described in detail the experience of "cosmic consciousness," an intense immersion in the oneness of the cosmos. He suggested that various historical luminaries were immersed in this state of mind, including the Gautama Buddha, Jesus Christ, William Blake, and Henry David Thoreau, and he hypothesized that their great influence and brilliant creativity stemmed from that "cosmic" awareness experience. Although intense or extreme versions of this altered state have been given different labels in different parts of the world (i.e., *samadhi*, *moksha*, enlightenment, rapture, transcendental awareness), there appears to be universal agreement that such experiences are both pleasing and capable of producing long-term beneficial changes (cf. White, 1972).

This state of undistracted, unself-conscious action and experience may seem ineffable and serendipitous in nature, but it can be simulated intentionally, as well. Havens (1982) investigated the use of hypnotic trance to stimulate approximations of "cosmic consciousness." Volunteers were guided through a graduated series of hypnotically induced alterations in experience over six 90-minute sessions. The procedure began with suggestions for increased awareness of thoughts and sensations and then gradually reduced awareness of all experience. The final session culminated in a symbolic dissolution/rebirth of the self, an experience that reportedly precedes most transcendental or cosmic consciousness episodes (cf. Masters & Houston, 1966, 1972). All participants found the process pleasant and all indicated a profound sense of calm and contentment. They also reported feeling more focused and effective in their everyday activities. Several indicated that the rebirth experience itself had been profoundly moving and had changed their perspective in significant ways.

The scripts presented below are examples of this "cosmic consciousness" approach. The first session focuses attention on an awareness of beauty and perfection in the events of the moment and seeks to remove all sense of self-conscious concerns. The second session offers a more extreme alteration in awareness. It encourages the individual to let go of all personal boundaries and to become immersed in the "energy of the cosmos" as the self dissolves and reemerges.

As with the meditation trances, it is advised that these experiences be reserved for people who are capable of enjoying and benefiting from them. Clients who have a tendency toward bizarre delusions or high levels of anxiety probably will not profit from such experiences. Also recognize that these scripts merely offer descriptive approximations of mystical states. They may be enlightening, but they will not produce enlightenment.

THE EAGLE'S EYE

A Trance for Enhanced Consciousness

And so,
as you continue to relax
and to drift,
like the drifting
of an eagle,
on the warm air rising
in columns of uplifting mist,
across the sands of time
in the deserts of the mind,
where all seems empty,
and yet full of colors
sparkling from below,
and white clouds float
across the sky
casting shadows on the ground,
and all it takes,
to turn and dive
or rise up higher
than before,
is a simple twist
of a wing tip here,
a small shift
of the tail there,
where the rising winds
catch the feathers
that ripple in the breeze,
feathers worn by the people
to honor those in the air,
where the red cliffs rise
far above the valley down
        below
and a clear blue river flows

in a winding, slithering path
with green on either side,
where trees and bushes hide
from the heat of the sand.
But flight is just the start
of the eagle's amazing grace
that carries you up and up
until they can barely see
from the ground
what it is up there,
because, you see, the eagle's
        eyes
are quite different
as it scans the ground.
It sees far and wide,
from thousands of yards away,
the tiniest leaf and twig below,
the smallest movement
of the smallest mouse
running beneath a bush,
its vision as sharp
as the talons on its feet,
sees every detail
from up on high.
Even the salmon in the river
cannot escape its stare
that focuses in like binoculars,
a crystal-clear point of view,
and sees the swimming dance
along the rocky waves
and centers its gaze
in that direction

while flying in large,
silent circles
high above.
With eyes so fine
you and I could truly see,
and nothing would escape
our notice,
drifting along above it all,
able to look and see,
a relaxed examination
of all there is and more,
a comfortable awareness,
like the warrior walking,
stalking,
in the silence of the trees,
hearing the breeze,
seeing the leaves
as they blow and move
while the animals scamper
through them,
always aware of everything
      there
alert and watching
with open eyes
and an open mind,
filling the woods
with awareness,
aware and waiting,
wearing the feathers
of the eagle in the sky
to remind you
to pay attention
and to see what there is to see,
to hear what there is to hear,
to be awake and be alert,
to let the mind move out
beyond the limits of the body,
the way the blind

learn to feel
with the tip of their cane
as if it were a finger,
extending their reach
several feet beyond their hand,
touching and feeling the
      street,
the curbs, the tables and
      chairs.
The mind and the body can
      reach
and see and feel
the way the eagle's can,
a thousand feet or more
beyond,
and the ears can hear
and expand the mind
to fill the room
or out the door
to explore the street
and every sound takes you
further out,
until you begin to touch
the walls, the ceiling, the floor,
and more,
the people breathe and move
      and speak
and take you in toward their
      unconscious,
where the eagle's eye can see
what they think and feel
and can explore those openings
that lead into the caves
where bats can fly
and find their nests
and mates
using only sound to guide
      them,

sound serving as eyes
to guide them,
and to guide us,
if we pay attention,
the guiding light appears
and lifts us like a feather
up toward the warmth
and the clear bright view
of the world out there
and the world in there
and pulls the film
back from our view,
the way the ancients
used to do
with their roots and dances
around the flames,
with drums and flutes
until they entered trances
that opened their eyes and
    ears
and let them truly see,
the kind of seeing
you can have
when you finally wake up
and let your eyes touch
the light,
your ears feel the sounds,
your mind touches the earth,
the way the eagle's do,
the filters pulled back
to let the light through
to let you see
and be awake
to the colors, shapes, and
    forms,

to let you see the texture
of the rug, the wood, the
    glass,
to let you feel them with your
    mind,
awake at last
to each small detail
and to the form and pattern,
the way an artist sees
and tries to capture on canvas,
the colors reflecting light,
the pattern of shapes and
    forms
as they dance in harmony
together
reaching out to us,
if only we can see,
the beauty there,
everywhere,
the way you see things
on vacation in a distant city
where each building jumps out
    at you
and each plant seems special,
and the mind becomes alert
to everything,
now,
even as you allow
that drifting up,
back to wakeful awareness,
back to brilliant alertness
of all there is,
eyes open
and wide awake
now.

THE PRINCE'S JOURNEY

A Metaphorical Search for Cosmic Awareness

And now,
as you continue to relax,
and pay close attention
to the things I am
saying,
you can recognize
the pleasure
of the anticipation
that something different
and wonderful
can happen to you.
You can wonder
how it will feel
to allow yourself
to experience
this wonderful difference,
even while you continue
to experience the comfort
and the effortlessness
of listening
and feeling
those events as they occur
without knowing
how it really was
to be that young prince,
who left the palace one day
to explore the kingdom
and was puzzled
by what he saw,
the good and the bad,
the pleasant and the sad,
and he wondered,

what life is,
and what the source was
of everything he saw,
and why do the birds
do what birds do,
fly, sing, soar on the wind,
or the fish swim
in silent ballets
of grace and beauty
while the water flows
through the smooth rocks
as the grasses dance
in the unseen wind
and the clouds drift
above it all,
being able,
more and more,
to learn what he learned
that day when,
like you,
he finally sat and rested
beneath a tree
of ancient size,
and sought the light
of wisdom,
as he quieted his mind
and drifted down
deeper and deeper,
going within,
to that calm, still place
where all is
stillness,

and there is no need
to make an effort
to pay close attention
to the position of the arms,
or the legs,
or the entire body,
and even the effort it takes
to pay close attention
to thoughts
or sensations
is too much effort
to bother making.
Just drifting down and
entering
that inner palace,
meeting
that inner self,
finding
that quiet core
of being there,
where the self continues,
now,
even when all else
drifts away from awareness
and there is nothing left
but the silent self . . .
a self
that has no form,
no shape,
no sound,
no thoughts,
no reasons to do
one thing or another,
just you
being you,
sitting there
quietly aware,
a self that may seem to be

a different self
from that prince's self
but may turn out to be
the same self later on,
as it disappears
from view,
and you disappear too
in a blank, black
nothingness,
though at first it
may be easier
or more difficult to find,
hiding deep within,
that small spark,
that sparkle,
that self that is the self
of all that is,
experiencing that energy
of that self now,
that calm buzzing energy
that is the self
of all that is,
that tingling, buzzing white
    light
of energy,
that grows brighter
as it surrounds the mind,
closer and closer,
becoming a blazing radiance
that envelops everything,
surrounds awareness with
    brightness,
a brilliant white brightness
that fills awareness,
and becomes everything you
    see . . .
everything you feel . . .
becomes what you hear . . .

what you taste . . . ,
becomes all there is
everyplace,
a blaze
of cool white bright light,
from the inner places
of all those spaces
where life is,
where everything is,
where the universe is,
the energy that dances
in everything everywhere,
the energy that is the mind,
and becomes thought,
becomes experience,
illuminates all
in that white light,
faint at first, perhaps,
just glimpses here and there,
a sensation in a hand,
a sparkle of light
off to the side,
a glow inside the mind,
and then a burst of bright
from the heart of the matter,
connecting each to all,
the dancing energy
of it all, of it all . . .
the heat of the sun,
the magic of the rainbow,
the power that flows
in the stars that glow
and dances in the rocks,
that bursts the waves
into sparkles of mist
and paints the flowers
with perfumes of lust
and guides the fish

as they weave the fabric
of life around the leaves
of trees,
the ancient tree of wisdom,
where the prince sat
and knew the energy
that comes as light,
while the chorus sings
a harmony of wordless sound,
all sounds from everywhere
that surround the mind
with the bright, brighter,
    brightest
bursts of white pure light,
and even the quietest night
becomes a loud joyful day
where the wings of snow
carry that feeling of love
and the brightest joy of all
is the laugh of a child
giggling on the grass,
tickled by puppies,
nibbling on ears
and licking the tart taste
of cherries and berries
from lips that sparkle
while the sounds of white light
dancing in the air
as the mind dissolves
and the body dissolves
like sugar
in bright warm water,
each sparkling tiny piece
floating away,
merging with the air,
spreading here and there
throughout the room,
throughout the air,

floating in space and time
everywhere, every time,
and in that time
finding that place
where it all joins together
everyplace
and becomes one
with it all,
one with all,
one . . .
one . . .
one quiet rhythm,
one silent pulse,
beating
throughout the world,
guiding everything,
in
and out,
in and out,
connecting
each to all,
feeling all within,
joining in life,
touching
the center
of your self,
becoming one
with the ocean
of being,
being one
with everything,
just being. . . .

And when the prince awoke
that day,
he looked around
and nothing seemed the same,
because at last he felt
awake,
truly awake,
to the beauties and wonder
of it all,
and as you awake,
you can begin to wonder
what it will be like
to see that bright white light
in everything you hear,
in everything you touch,
and in everything that touches
      you
as you drift up toward the
      surface
of wakeful awareness now,
more and more awake,
until eventually
you reach that point
where it is comfortable
to allow the eyes to open
and to return to conscious
      awareness
quite completely.
That's right,
eyes open
and wide awake
now.

13

UNCONSCIOUS RESOURCES

The unconscious mind contains understandings and abilities that we ordinarily do not have available at the conscious level. These unconscious capacities can be accessed in two different ways. Erickson's request to his own unconscious,"Unconscious, do your stuff"(Erickson & Rossi, 1977, p. 47), nicely summarizes one of these approaches, that is, a simple request to the unconscious for help. Rossi (1986) also used this approach. He recommended that the hypnotized subject focus on the nature of the problem, consider potential solutions, and ask his or her unconscious to solve the difficulty or accomplish the goal. The subject is then asked to step aside, so to speak, and to wait for the unconscious to signal that it has finished its work.

Erickson also accessed unconscious resources by establishing a direct line of communication for the unconscious mind, such as finger signals and automatic writing. Cheek (1962) employed a swinging pendulum for this purpose, instructing the unconscious to swing the pendulum in one direction for "Yes" and in the other for "No." Rossi (1986) recommended the use of the "voice of the mind/body" (p. 191) to communicate directly with the unconscious. This unconscious inner voice, referred to by Hilgard (1977) as the "hidden observer," gives the unconscious a straightforward means of communication to the client's conscious mind. Bresler (1990) encouraged his patients to find an imaginary object or animal through which the unconscious may speak to the conscious mind. This internal representation of a being who speaks with great wisdom sounds very similar to the "spirits"contacted by the Sioux medicine man Lame Deer for assistance and guidance (Fire & Erdoes, 1972) and to the "spirit guides" described by Samuels and Bennett (1974).

Two scripts are presented below. The first asks the subject to clarify his or her goals and then to let the unconscious take over. The second illustrates the use of trance to create an internal representation of the unconscious, a "guide." Once created or found, this guide can be consulted at any time for advice, comfort, and problem solving.

LET THE GENIE DO IT

A Trance for Releasing Unconscious Potentials

And now,
as you drift
in that letting go,
you may become
even more aware
that you have a conscious mind,
and an **unconscious** mind,
an inner self,
a *quiet* self,
hidden deep within,
that becomes more available
as you drift down.
And this inner mind,
this unconscious mind,
has many abilities
and understandings
that you can use
to become more comfortable,
to become happier,
to enjoy your life
more fully,
because your unconscious mind
can think about these goals,
can understand how it would
    feel
to be there now,
being more able
to be that way,
to think that way,
to feel that way,
and when it knows
what it can do
to help you,

you may realize it too
because it can show you
a thought,
a memory,
a sensation, or an image
that at first may seem unusual,
but later on turns out
to be your unconscious
telling you,
it knows what to do
and how,
to free you in that way,
to help you in that way,
and I don't know,
and you don't know,
what it knows
or what it will do
for you,
but I do know
that you can wait
now
for your inner self
to review that goal,
to find those thoughts,
those new ways of doing,
those memories of learning,
that meet those needs,
that accomplish those goals.
And when it is through,
when it knows what to do,
when it recognizes how to use
your own experiences,
your own reactions,

your own way of doing things
to help you accomplish those
    things
you want it to,
you need it to,
that are so good for you,
you can know it is through
thinking about things,
and it knows what to do,
and it will do it for you,
because you will begin to drift
back toward the surface
of normal, wakeful
alertness,
back toward the surface
where you can feel yourself
wanting to open your eyes
    then,
when it is ready to do
what it can do
to help you enjoy
being you,
being here and now,
feeling good about you

and many other things too,
as you wait here now
for it to decide
what to do and when
and then,
when your unconscious knows
and is ready to do
what can be good for you
you can open your eyes
then,
and return
to comfortable,
wakeful alertness,
wondering what and when
you will first begin
to notice those changes
in you.
That's right,
just waiting,
and when it is right,
your eyes can open
and you can awaken
quite completely
now.

PRIVATE GUIDES

A Trance for Contacting the Unconscious Mind

Drifting down within,
into a deeper trance than
    before,
it becomes easier
and easier to let go
and to allow the mind
to float down on its own,
down toward the floor

of that place
of quiet calm awareness
that almost seems
to give off signals
that guide and direct
attention down toward it,
down toward that place
of effortless letting go,

a peaceful place,
a safe place to be
as the mind drifts free
and gradually becomes aware
of what that place is like
down there,
that place where you may
have been before,
your own private place
of peace and calm,
a serene place to be
that provides more and more
of an awareness
that you have been here
before.
And I don't know
exactly what that place
is like for you,
but I do know
that it can find you
as you relax
and allow it to,
because after a while
it becomes clearer
and clearer . . .
the sights,
the sounds,
even the smells
that seem to surround
are quite familiar,
a place that comes to mind
automatically
when you drift toward
that feeling
of deep, calm peacefulness,
which for some people
is a quiet pond
set deep in the woods

where all is silent and still,
and for others
is a sandy beach
that the ocean
slides shells upon
with a soothing, rhythmic
     roar.
And so you take your own time
to find that place inside your
     mind
where that memory of a peace-
     ful time
allows the mind to find
that image of that special
     place,
the sounds of that special place,
the feelings felt within that
     place,
and then to move
within that place
and to be there now
can allow you to experience
the pleasure of that treasure
within,
a comforting place to be,
where you are free
to explore and feel
the safety felt before,
a vacation from it all,
where you have been before.
But as you go there now,
again,
and begin to look around,
remember to remember
the ancient lore
told by mystics
and the members of many
     tribes

that hidden down deep inside,
down within that special place,
everyone has a guide,
an inner voice that all can find
that will tell them
what is on their mind,
that knows more than they
can see
and wants to share
and will come out
within that silence there
and reveal itself
to those who stand and wait
and listen to that silence
for the message,
like the warriors
who go on a long journey
to find that guide inside
and may find a wolf
that speaks a name,
or a bird that thinks thoughts,
or the Zulu
who talks to clouds
and hears the truth
spoken by ancestors gone
    before,
their voices blending with the
    wind
and the charming tales
of talking rocks
that offer thoughts
and understandings
that few would otherwise
    admit.
So go forth now,
as you let go,
and search those inner spaces
for your inner guide

that lives in there
and waits to take you places
in your understandings,
waits to answer questions
about anything you wish,
tries in dreams
to tell you things
that often go ignored,
and serves you like a genie
placed in the lamp of life
where wisdom and
    understanding
frequently are stored.
Once you find it,
that inner guide inside
is always there,
waiting there,
waiting for your return,
waiting to provide
ideas and understandings,
waiting to guide you
where you want to go,
so search for it now
by sitting still
and looking around inside
and talk to it
and listen to it
and let its wisdom
be your guide.
That's right,
ask its name . . . ,
hear its message . . . ,
let it talk to you. . . .

(*Pause for a minute or two.*)

Now,
let it become your symbol,
a punctuation mark of sound

or a captivating image
that catches your attention
and orchestrates awareness
whenever it comes to mind,
whether what you found
to be your guide
was a crystal or a flower,
an animal or a person
who lived and learned before,
whatever it is for you
get to know it now
and whenever you want
    more,
just go inside again
and look around for it,
knowing it is there
and speak to it and ask it
whatever you want it to share,
and listen to its message,
perhaps a voice is there,
or just a thought,
or a silent memory,
or even an image
of what the message is,
because it knows
and so will you,
when you go there

to find it
and welcome it
into your thoughts,
a welcome relief
to have a guide
hidden deep inside,
a pleasant recognition,
even as you say goodbye
to it now,
and thank it for showing
    itself
to you now,
and remember where and how
to find it
even as you leave it
and drift back up
toward the surface of
    awareness,
gradually leaving that special
    place
where you met that guide
and returning to the world
    outside
as wakeful alertness returns
quite comfortably and
    completely,
now.

14

WRITING YOUR OWN HYPNOSIS SCRIPTS

Early in his career, Erickson wrote out scripts for upcoming sessions. He then spent hours reducing many pages of suggestions to one or two, all the while attempting to amplify the essence of his original message (Erickson, 1976, in Rossi, 1980, Vol.I, p. 489). He also recommended this procedure to his students, stating that it would sensitize them to the associative content and implications of each word, phrase, or pause they might employ during the trance process.

A script also gives you a prearranged structure to follow throughout the hypnotherapeutic process. We find that both novices and advanced hypnotherapists experience less "performance anxiety" when they use a script (cf. Havens & Walters, 1989b). Instead of searching for the "right" words on the spot, your script is your guide.

The scripts presented in this book give you an opportunity to rehearse hypnotic induction procedures and to familiarize yourself with direct and indirect suggestions. As you become comfortable with the hypnotic skills presented in our scripts, however, you will want to create your own scripts. Not only will this sensitize you to the multiple uses and meanings of words, but it also will enable you to incorporate your own style into the process and to adjust your wording to meet the specific needs or interests of each unique client. As you observe your subject closely for signs of relaxation or restlessness throughout the session, your observations will tell you immediately what parts of your script are working and what parts are not.

It is relatively easy to create a trance script. We suggest that you begin simply by writing out a basic induction. Keep in mind that your goal is to capture attention, hold it steady for a few minutes, and then redirect it toward a particular hypnotic response of some sort. To do this, you will start with a few statements that reflect what the subject is actually doing and possibly is experiencing at that very moment. This will capture the subject's attention and reassure him or her that what is happening is what is supposed to happen. Next, you will begin to weave in metaphorical and direct suggestions about other things that might enter attention. These "other things" will be thoughts, sensations, and perceptions that are somehow related to the hypnotic response you are attempting to create. Thus you want to start by describing what the person is paying attention to at the time and then gradually redirect that attention toward something different, something you select.

Presented in the following are step-by-step instructions for constructing induction and suggestion sessions similar to those presented in this text. You may also wish to refer to our induction scripts in Chapter 4 for additional guidance and inspiration.

STEPS IN CONSTRUCTING SESSIONS

Step 1: Setting Goals

Determine, with the client, as exactly as possible, his or her goals. What does the client expect to learn and/or achieve using hypnosis? Once you and the client have specified goals, you are ready to begin writing your own hypnotherapy scripts.

Write down each of your client's goals. Next to each goal, describe the particular change(s) in attitudes or behavior you believe might be necessary to accomplish that goal. Also note any resources you believe the client may have that pertain to each goal. For example, if your client lives a high-stress life and his or her goals are centered on relaxation, you would note potential attitude and/or behavior changes that are typically associated with relaxation. You would also note the activities (e.g., fishing and sailing) that the client has found to be relaxing in the past.

Because it is a bit presumptuous to assume that the therapist is always (or ever) in a position to determine accurately the best way for a client to accomplish a goal, your list of client resources should always end with "unconscious mind." This will remind you that it often is best to leave the selection of appropriate avenues of change entirely up to the subject's unconscious. To do this, simply explain the client's goals to the unconscious in a straightforward manner during the trance and encourage it to respond in whatever fashion it decides will be the most useful. It is efficacious to solicit this unconscious source of change even when you have a definite idea about the best ways and means to accomplish the client's goals hypnotically.

Step 2: Selecting Direct or Indirect Suggestions

Now that you have determined your client's goals and possible resources for accomplishing those goals, it is time to decide whether to use direct or indirect suggestions for change. In some instances, you will be able to ask your hypnotized client to make the desired changes *directly*, clearly describing the changes needed and offering direct suggestions regarding the accomplishment of these changes. This approach is useful with clients who are highly responsive to the hypnosis process and offer no resistance to the changes suggested. In other cases, perhaps the majority, an indirect approach will prove to be the most effective. An indirect approach relies on metaphorical anecdotes to guide the client in the direction of change. This approach bypasses conscious resistance because it conveys the message about suggested alterations indirectly. Generally, it is advisable to include both direct and indirect suggestions.

Step 3: Constructing Direct Suggestions

Now, using your list of client goals, write out several sentences that directly instruct the subject to change in the direction of his or her desired outcome. For example, "When you leave here today you can notice that you feel unusually rested and calm." This would be an appropriate direct suggestion for a highly stressed client.

Although your instructions to the subject can be straightforward, it is good to avoid words or phrases that are overtly authoritarian. For example, instead of saying, "You *will* do X, Y, or Z," you might say, "You *can* or *may* do X, Y,or Z." You may use the following examples to guide your wording.

"Now, I wonder if you can . . ."
"Naturally, it will be easy for you to . . ."
"I want you to see how well you can . . ."
"If you pay close attention, you may notice that you are able
    to . . ."
"Eventually, you may discover that you can . . ."

Such wordings offer direct suggestions for a specific response, yet they do so in a relatively gentle and seemingly permissive manner. They enable the hypnotherapist to make direct requests for a response without straightforwardly challenging the client. Many people believe, erroneously, that hypnosis is some sort of "mind control," but most subjects will respond to authoritarian demands with resistance and noncompliance.

Step 4: Constructing Indirect Suggestions (Metaphors)

A. *Selecting metaphors and anecdotes related to the client's current situation and goals.* Construct a list of metaphorical terms and stories that are in some way related to the client's current situation or stated goals. These metaphors may come from the words the client uses to discuss his or her feelings about the situation. For example, a client may talk about feeling "stuck" or "mired down," terms that suggest such things as quicksand, flypaper, tar, gum, and mud. Other topics for metaphorical anecdotes may be derived from your own associations to the client's goals or even to the client's dominant physical or behavioral features. One client may remind you of a teddy bear, while the far-reaching goals of another client may bring images of travel to mind. Write down whatever comes to mind as you ponder the client's characteristics, interests, situation, and goals.

B. *Identifying the metaphors to be used.* Look over the list of terms or topics that you have now identified as somehow related metaphorically to a particular client. As you read through the list, locate those that remind you of a story about another client, an event from your past, a natural event, or an animal. For example, if one of the words on the list happened to be "magnifying glass," you might be reminded of a story from your childhood about using a magnifying glass to burn holes in a leaf, about a friend who uses a magnifying glass to study the engravings on the stamps he collects, or about a grandparent who used a magnifying glass to read the newspaper. Select two or three metaphors that seem to stimulate the most interesting stories for you and underline them.

C. *Creating relevant puns, plays on words, rhymes, and multiple interconnections.* Pick one of the metaphors you underlined above. Write a list of all the terms you can think of that relate to that underlined word. Continuing with the "magnifying glass" metaphor, we might generate a list that contains the following key words: focus, lens, enlarge, details, beams of light, clear, concentrate, examine, and read. Now, for each of these associated key words or phrases, write out as many different possible uses or meanings as you can. "Concentrate," for example, might be used to refer to a concentration of attention, a mix for an orange drink, or a gathering together of resources in one particular place. Repeat this process with the other underlined metaphors, identifying key words or phrases and finding multiple meanings of those words. Finally, add a list of words that rhyme with these metaphor-relevant terms. "Concentrate," for example, rhymes with such words as contemplate, consecrate, consolidate, elaborate, and integrate, each of which is a potentially meaningful term in a hypnotherapy context.

D. *Writing metaphorical anecdotes.* Write out a story for each of the metaphors on which you have been working. Give it a beginning that relates in some way to the client's current situation, a middle that elaborates the details, and an ending that involves an accomplishment relevant to the goals of the client. Writing three to six words per line will help you to maintain a slow rhythm as you speak. Connect phrase after phrase with words such as "and," "or," and "also" to maintain a sense of continuous flow. Periodically, work in one of the key words or phrases you identified in the foregoing step as being related to the original metaphor, and then use the same word in a different context in the very next line. You may wish to use a rhyming word soon afterward. This adds an interesting and captivatingly confusing complexity to your presentation and further depotentiates conscious mental sets.

At first, writing out a metaphorical anecdote may seem a difficult or confusing business. However, if you allow your creative juices to flow, engage in some free association, and use our scripts as guidelines, you will soon discover that captivating words and phrases emerge effortlessly from your mind. Think of it as writing poetry or song lyrics and it becomes a challenging, multileveled esthetic game—that is, the use of symbolic words, images, and sounds to stimulate growth-enhancing thoughts and recognitions in someone else.

Step 5: Writing Your Trance Script

A. *Begin your hypnotic induction/suggestion script with several sentences that describe the current physical position and probable ongoing experiences of the subject.* These should be relatively simple statements such as the following: "You are sitting in a relaxed position." "Your arms are at your sides." "Your eyes are closed." "You may be wondering what will happen next." "You may be more aware of some things than you were before." Each of these will be heard as a simple statement of fact, an accurate description of things at that moment.

B. *After several descriptive statements, insert a sentence that leads the person toward a hypnotic response.* The purely descriptive statements you use at the beginning of your induction script help to establish cooperative rapport and demonstrate to the client that you know what he or she is experiencing. Now is the time to use a question or statement that guides the subject toward a hypnotic response that might not occur or enter awareness unless you mention it. For example, you could wonder if the subject has noticed the beginnings of a feeling of heaviness in a hand, or you could point out a slight feeling of tingling in a leg or a finger that continues to grow over time. You can suggest modifications of virtually any sensory experience in whatever direction you choose, but always remember to give the subject plenty of options. "Either the right hand or the left hand may feel heavier or lighter as you drift down deeper." Use your own imagination to point out possible hypnotic experiences that will fascinate the person and offer additional evidence that trance is developing.

C. *Begin to alternate descriptive and suggestive statements, gradually increasing the frequency of the suggestive, leading comments.* As you proceed with the induction, begin to intersperse more and more sentences that briefly describe experiences commonly associated with hypnosis. When subjects begin searching for such experiences, this increases the likelihood that they will occur and that a trance will develop as a result. Such comments as, "You may be able to notice a drifting down, a gradual letting go that allows a trance to continue to develop," will facilitate the development of a trance, as will such statements as, "There is a growing sense of comfort as you realize that your own unconscious mind can be allowed to do things for you."

Continue to insert a descriptively accurate statement every now and then, but gradually increase the frequency of your leading comments until you have described the subjective experiences of relaxation, effortless awareness, and comfort commonly associated with a trance. Your induction may also include any dissociative hypnotic experiences you hope to elicit as well (inability to move, automatic movement of an arm or finger, an auditory or kinesthetic hallucination, a distorted sense of time or place, entry into an imaginary reality, etc.).

D. *Following the induction, insert one or two metaphors.* Use the metaphorical anecdote you wrote in step 4(D) that you feel has the least obvious relevance to the goals of your client or is the story most likely to be of most interest to that person. The idea is to begin with something that will hold the subject's interest without disrupting the trance state of mind. If you begin with a metaphor that has an obvious relevance to the concerns of the subject, you may provoke a conscious critique and a reorienting response. The client may begin to listen in a critical or analytic manner and emerge from the trance.

Every now and then, weave a trance-maintenance suggestion into the metaphor by saying something like, "And as you wonder what happened next, you may find yourself drifting even deeper, becoming more comfortable, just as Grandma did when. . . ." This will help the subject to reestablish or deepen the trance while remaining comfortably observant. When you have finished presenting this metaphor, you may either present your direct suggestions and then terminate the trance session or make a transition into another, more directly suggestive, metaphor. Multiple metaphors can be presented during a session, time permitting, and can be combined or intertwined in complex ways. On the other hand, one metaphorical anecdote can be sufficient.

E. *Add several direct suggestions for the same changes implied by your metaphor.* Metaphorical anecdotes offer the subject a suggested course of action in analogical or symbolic fashion. Although is not necessary to point out "the moral of the story" at the end of a metaphorical anecdote, this is an appropriate place to incorporate one or two of the direct suggestions you wrote in step 3. It also is an appropriate time to request that the client's unconscious mind find its own way to accomplish the goals and to suggest that it integrate the things learned during the trance.

F. *Once you have added your metaphorical and direct suggestions, it is time to create a few comments that will gently reintroduce your client to conscious awareness.* Trance termination comments usually do not have to be extensive. Simply indicate that it is time to end the session, that the subject can begin to reorient to a normal state of wakeful alertness, and that he or she will feel fine afterward. There is no set way to end a trance session. Each of our trance scripts ends a bit differently, some in a rather abrupt termination and some in a lengthy reorientation. We do recommend that you use a similar ending each time you do trance work with the same client. This repetition gives the individual an easily identifiable cue that the session is ending and encourages the reorientation process.

OUTGROWING SCRIPTS

Writing out hypnotherapy scripts makes it easier to explore the many entrancing and suggestive possibilities of language and cooperative interpersonal communication. Your goal is to become so familiar with the verbal and conceptual constructions involved that you will no longer need a script to do it well. You will become adept at facilitating trance states and comfortable with creating metaphors and suggestions, able to modify and invent what you say in response to the needs and reactions of your clients. As this happens, you will become immersed in the ongoing flow of events and feel a sense of direct connection to the experiences of the subject. This entry into the trance realm with a client provides a personal, experientially based source of guidance that transcends instructions we or others can provide. Writing your own scripts is a direct route to this goal.

POSTSCRIPT

Trance is a universally attainable state of mind. During trance, people are open to new ideas and are willing to allow themselves to have unusual experiences and responses. Hypnosis offers access to unconscious potentials and enables subjects to use resources that otherwise might go to waste or even be misused. Unfortunately, hypnotic abilities can be misused unintentionally simply because most people are unaware of their own trance tendencies (cf. Wolinsky & Ryan, 1991). Hypnosis also can be misused and/or abused by lay hypnotists who lack the clinical training and ethical prohibitions of professional therapists. As professionals become more familiar with the hypnotic experience and begin to teach more people how to use their own trance abilities, these problems will be alleviated. The mystery and mystique surrounding this natural human talent will diminish and the potentials unveiled by this state of mind will become a widely available part of our wellness regimen. Until that time, each hypnotherapist has a special privilege and a special responsibility. We have the privilege of entering into a uniquely open and cooperative relationship with many people, each of whom teaches us more about the remarkable capacities of the human mind. We have a responsibility to use these relationships to enhance the welfare of our clients and to protect the integrity of each individual.

We encourage you to expand the scope and orientation of your practice to include the search for the attitudes and actions that contribute to wellness, tranquillity, and peak performance. We also encourage you to expand your definition of the populations you serve and the format you use to serve them. The opportunity to learn how to use hypnotic trance to modify attention and experience in specific ways can be used by people to enhance their performance in educational, business, and sports settings. It also can provide access to more productive, pleasurable, and healthy styles of thinking and living.

But the attention management skills offered by hypnotic trance are a possible source of personal enrichment for many more people than can be served on a one-to-one basis. Although we would never recommend using group trance sessions for psychotherapeutic purposes, this seems to be a viable format for training in attention management and for the enhancement of well-being. Erickson himself frequently closed conferences and workshops with group inductions (e.g., Erickson, 1965). The potential utility of such a strategy also is reflected in the fact that Havens and Dimond (1978) found that 93 percent of their subjects reported hypnotic responses following an Ericksonian-style group induction and none reported negative effects.

Hypnotherapy is a process of discovery and liberation. When our clients learn to use trance to manage their attention, they are delighted with the array of resources they discover within themselves. Discovering inner resources is a liberating experience and a catalyst for wellness, tranquillity, and peak performance. It gives the phrase "pay attention" a brand-new meaning.

REFERENCES

Abramson, L. Y., & Alloy, L. B. (1981). Depression, non-depression and cognitive "illusions": A reply to Schwartz. *Journal of Experimental Psychology, 110*, 436–437.

Adams, J. L. (1974). *Conceptual blockbusting: A pleasurable guide to better problem solving.* San Francisco: San Francisco Book Co.

Alloy, L. B., Abramson, L. Y., & Viscusi, D. (1981). Induced mood and the illusion of control. *Journal of Personality and Social Psychology, 41*, 1129–1140.

American Psychiatric Association (1987). *Diagnostic and statistical manual of mental disorders* (3rd ed., rev.), Washington, DC: Author.

Anooshian, L. J. (1989). Effects of attentive encoding on analytic and nonanalytic processing in implicit and explicit retrieval tasks. *Bulletin of Psychonomic Society, 27*, 5–8.

Atkinson, J. W., & Feather, N. T. (Eds.) (1966). *A theory of achievement motivation.* New York: Wiley.

Bandura, A., Taylor, C. B., Williams, L. W., Mefford, I. N., & Barchas, J. D. (1985). Catecholamine secretion as a function of perceived coping self-efficacy. *Journal of Consulting and Clinical Psychology, 53*, 406–414.

Barber, T. X. (1960). The necessary and sufficient conditions for hypnotic behavior. *American Journal of Clinical Hypnosis, 3*, 31–42.

Barker, P. A. (1985). *Using metaphors in psychotherapy.* New York: Brunner/Mazel.

Bartlett, F. C. (1932). *Remembering.* Cambridge, England: Cambridge University Press.

Bateson, G. (1972). *Steps to an ecology of mind.* New York: Ballantine.

Bateson, G. (1979). *Mind and nature: A necessary unity.* New York: Dutton.

Benson, H. (1975). *The relaxation response.* New York: Morrow.

Bonny, H., & McCarron, N. (1984). Music as an adjunct to anesthesia in operative procdures. *AANA Journal, 52,* 55–57.

Boostrom, R. (1992). *Developing creative and critical thinking: An integrated approach.* Lincolnwood, IL: National Textbook.

Bornstein, M. H., & Ruddy, M. G. (1984). Infant attention and maternal stimulation: Prediction of cognitive and linguistic development in singletons and twins. In H. Bouma & D. G. Bouwhuis (Eds.), *Attention and performance X: Control of language processes* (pp. 433-445). Hillsdale, NJ: Erlbaum.

Bresler, D. E. (1990). Meeting an inner adviser. In D.C. Hammond (Ed.), *Handbook of hypnotic suggestions and metaphors* (pp. 318–320). New York: Norton.

Broadbent, D. E. (1958). *Perception and communication.* New York: Pergamon.

Brody, R. (1986). The sweet science of smell. *American Health, 5,* 55–60.

Bucke, R. M. (1900). *Cosmic consciousness: A study in the evolution of the human mind.* New York: Causeway.

Callahan, D. (1990). *What kind of life: The limits of medical progress.* New York: Touchstone.

Cautela, J. R. (1966). Treatment of compulsive behavior by covert sensitization. *Psychological Record, 16,* 33–41.

Cautela, J. R. (1967). Covert sensitization. *Psychological Reports, 20,* 459–468.

Cautela, J. R. (1973). Covert processes and behavior modification. *Journal of Nervous and Mental Disease, 157,* 27–35.

Cheek, D. (1962). Some applications of hypnosis and ideomotor questioning for analysis and therapy in medicine. *American Journal of Clinical Hypnosis, 5,* 92–104.

Conze, E. (1975). *Buddhism: Its essence and development.* New York: Harper Torchbooks.

Cowan, N. (1988). Evolving conceptions of memory storage, selective attention and their mutual constraints within the human information processing system. *Psychological Bulletin, 104,* 163–191.

Crawford, J. (1985). The effects of hypnosis on immunity in humans.

Unpublished doctoral dissertation, University of Texas Health Science Center, Dallas.

Csikszentmihalyi, M. (1978). Attention and the holistic approach to behavior. In K. S. Pope & J. L. Singer (Eds.), *The stream of consciousness: Scientific investigations into the flow of human experiences* (pp. 335–358). New York: Plenum.

Csikszentmihalyi, M. (1990). *Flow: The psychology of optimal experience*. New York: Harper & Row.

Davidson, R. J., & Goleman, D. J. (1977). The role of attention in meditation and hypnosis: A psychobiological perspective on transformations of consciousness. *International Journal of Clinical and Experimental Hypnosis, 25*, 291–308.

Deikman, A. (1966). Deautomatization and the mystic experience. *Psychiatry, 29*, 324–338.

Dillon, K. M., Minchoff, B., & Baker, K. H. (1985). Positive emotional states and the enhancement of the immune system. *International Journal of Psychiatry in Medicine, 15*, 13–17.

Dixon, P. (1971). *Rhetoric*. London: Methuen.

Dolan, Y. M. (1986). Metaphors for motivation and intervention. *Family Therapy Collections, 19*, 1–10.

Egeth, H., & Bevan, W. (1973). Attention. In B. J. Wolman (Ed.), *Handbook of general psychology* (pp. 395–418). Englewood Cliffs, NJ: Prentice-Hall.

Epstein, M. (1990). Psychodynamics of meditation: Pitfalls on the spiritual path. *Journal of Transpersonal Psychology, 22*, 17–34.

Epstein, S., & Meier, P. (1989). Constructive thinking: A broad coping variable with distinctive components. *Journal of Personality and Social Psychology, 57*, 332–350.

Erickson, M. H. (1954). Special techniques of brief hypnotherapy. *Journal of Clinical and Experimental Hypnosis, 2*, 109–129.

Erickson, M. H. (Speaker) (1965, July). *General considerations in hypnosis* (cassette recording). The Milton H. Erickson Classic Cassette Series. Des Plaines, IL: American Society of Clinical Hypnosis.

Erickson, M. H. (1966). The interspersal hypnotic technique for symptom correction and pain control. *American Journal of Clinical Hypnosis, 8*, 198–209.

Erickson, M. H., (1980). *The collected papers of Milton H. Erickson on hypnosis* (E. L. Rossi, Ed.). New York: Irvington.

Erickson, M. H., & Rossi, E. (1977). Autohypnotic experiences of Milton H. Erickson. *American Journal of Clinical Hypnosis, 20*, 36–54.

Erickson, M. H., & Rossi, E. L. (1979). *Hypnotherapy: An exploratory casebook*. New York: Irvington.

Erickson, M. H., & Rossi, E. L. (1981). *Experiencing hypnosis: Therapeutic approaches to altered states*. New York: Irvington.

Erickson, M. H., Rossi, E. L., & Rossi, S. I. (1976). *Hypnotic realities: The induction of clinical hypnosis and forms of indirect suggestion*. New York: Irvington.

Erikson, E. (1963). *Childhood and society* (2nd ed.). New York: Norton.

Erikson, E. (1968). *Youth, identity and crisis*. New York: Norton.

Fantz, R. E. (1983). The use of metaphor and fantasy as an additional exploration of awareness. *Gestalt Journal, 6*, 28–33.

Fire, J., & Erdoes, R. (1972). *Lame Deer, seeker of visions*. New York: Simon & Schuster.

Flesch, R. (1951). *The art of clear thinking*. New York: Harper & Row.

Fodor, J. A. (1983). *The modularity of the mind*. Cambridge, MA: MIT Press.

Frank, J. (1963). *Persuasion and healing: A comparative study of psychotherapy*. New York: Schocken.

Fromm, E. (1941). *Escape from freedom*. New York: Rinehart.

Fromm, E. (1979). The nature of hypnosis and other altered states of consciousness. In E. Fromm & R. E. Shor (Eds.), *Hypnosis: Developments in research and new perspectives* (2nd ed.) (pp. 81–103). Hawthorne, NY: Aldine.

Fromm, E., & Shor, R. E. (Eds.) (1979). *Hypnosis: Developments in research and new perspectives* (2nd ed.). Hawthorne, NY: Aldine.

Gallwey, W. T. (1974). *The inner game of tennis*. New York: Random House.

Gazzaniga, M. S. (1983). Right hemisphere language following brain bisection: A 20-year perspective. *American Psychologist, 38*, 525–537.

Gill, M. M., & Brenman, M. (1961). *Hypnosis and related states*. New York: International Universities Press.

Gilligan, C. (1982). *In a different voice*. Cambridge, MA: Harvard University Press.

Gilligan, S. (1987). *Therapeutic trances: The cooperation principle in Ericksonian hypnotherapy*. New York: Brunner/Mazel.

Goleman, D. (1977). *The varieties of the meditative experience.* New York: Irvington.

Goleman, D., & Davidson, J. D. (Eds.) (1979). *Consciousness: Brain, states of awareness, and mysticism.* New York: Harper & Row.

Gordon, D. (1978). *Therapeutic metaphors.* Cupertino, CA: Meta.

Growald, E. R., & Luks, P. (1988). The immunity of Samaritans: Beyond the self. *American Health, 24,* 51–53.

Haley, J. (1973). *Uncommon therapy: The psychiatric techniques of Milton H. Erickson, M.D..* New York: Norton.

Haley, J. (1985). *Conversations with Milton H. Erickson, M.D.* New York: Triangle.

Hall, C. R. (1965). The influence of the mind on the body. In R. E. Shor & M. T. Orne (Eds.), *The nature of hypnosis* (pp. 42–52). New York: Holt, Rinehart & Winston.

Hanson, V. (1973). *Approaches to meditation.* Wheaton, IL: Quest.

Harris, T. G. (1989). Heart and soul. *Psychology Today, 23*(1), 50–51.

Hastorf, A. H., & Cantril, H. (1954). They saw a game: A case study. *Journal of Abnormal and Social Psychology, 49,* 129–134.

Havens, R. A. (1982). Approaching cosmic consciousness via hypnosis. *Journal of Humanistic Psychology, 22,* 105–116.

Havens, R. A. (1985a). Erickson vs. the establishment: Which won? In J. K. Zeig (Ed.), *Ericksonian psychotherapy* (Vol. 1, pp. 52–61). New York: Brunner/Mazel.

Havens, R. A. (1985b). *The wisdon of Milton H. Erickson.* New York: Irvington.

Havens, R. A. (1991, April). Trance and "flow": Results of an Ericksonian attempt to teach subjects how to use hypnosis to attain the state of focused attention Csikszentmihalyi has identified as the basis for optimal performance and tranquility. Paper presented at the American Society of Clinical Hypnosis 33rd Annual Scientific Meeting, St. Louis.

Havens, R. A., & Dimond, R. E. (1978, April). Preliminary norms on an Ericksonian approach: The Havens-Dimond hypnotic response scale. Paper presented at the American Society of Clinical Hypnosis 20th Annual Scientific Meeting, St. Louis.

Havens, R. A., & Walters, C. (1986, May). Empirical analysis of terms used by Milton H. Erickson to describe patients. Paper presented at the Midwestern Psychological Association Convention, Chicago.

Havens, R. A., & Walters, C. (presenters) (1989a). *An orientation to the trance experience* (cassette recording). New York: Brunner/Mazel.

Havens, R. A., & Walters, C. (1989b). *Hypnotherapy scripts: A neo-Ericksonian approach to persuasive healing.* New York: Brunner/Mazel.

Hayano, D. M. (1988). Dealing with chance: Self-deception and fantasy among gamblers. In J. S. Lockard & D. L. Paulhus (Eds.), *Self-deception: An adaptive mechanism?* (pp. 186–199). Englewood Cliffs, NJ: Prentice-Hall.

Herrigel, E. (1971). *Zen in the art of archery.* New York: Vintage.

Hilgard, E. R. (1965). *Hypnotic susceptibility.* New York: Harcourt, Brace & World.

Hilgard, E. R. (1977). *Divided consciousness: Multiple controls in human thought and action.* New York: Wiley.

Hilgard, J. (1979). Imaginative and sensory-affective involvements in everyday life and in hypnosis. In E. Fromm & R. E. Shor (Eds.), *Hypnosis: Developments in research and new perspectives* (pp. 483–517). Hawthorne, NY: Aldine.

Holmes, D. (1991). *Abnormal psychology.* New York: HarperCollins.

House, J. S., Landis, K. R., & Umberson, D. (1988). Social relationships and health. *Science, 241,* 540–545.

Hull, C. L. (1933). *Hypnosis and suggestibility.* New York: Appleton-Century-Crofts.

James, W. (1890). *Principles of psychology.* New York: Holt.

Kabat-Zinn, J. (1990). *Full catastrophe living: Using the wisdom of your body and mind to face stress, pain and illness.* New York: Delta.

Kaplan, G. A., & Comacho, T. (1983). Perceived health and mortality: A nine-year follow-up of the human population laboratory cohort. *American Journal of Epidemiology, 11,* 292–304.

Keele, S. W. (1973). *Attention and human performance.* Pacific Palisades, CA: Goodyear.

Kiecolt-Glaser, J. K., & Glaser, R. (1988). Behavioral influences on immune function: Evidence for the interplay between stress and health. In T. Field, P. McCabe, & N. Schneiderman (Eds.), *Stress and coping* (Vol. 2, pp. 105–139). Hillsdale, NJ: Erlbaum.

Klatzky, R. L. (1984). *Memory and awareness: An information-processing perspective.* New York: Freeman.

Kobasa, S. C., Maddi, S. R., & Kahn, S. (1982). Hardiness and health: A prospective study. *Journal of Personality and Social Psychology, 42*, 168–177.

Kroger, W. S., & Fezler, W. D. (1976). *Hypnosis and behavior modification: Imagery conditioning.* Philadelphia,: Lippincott.

LaBerge, D. L. (1991). Attention. *Psychological Science, 1*, 156–162.

Langer, E. J., & Roth, J. (1975). Heads I win, tails it's chance: The illusion of control and function of outcomes in a purely chance task. *Journal of Personality and Social Psychology, 34*, 191–198.

Lankton, S. R., & Lankton, C. H. (1983). *The answer within: A clinical framework of Ericksonian hypnotherapy.* New York: Brunner/Mazel.

Lankton, S. R., & Lankton, C. H. (1986). *Enchantment and intervention in family therapy: Training in Ericksonian hypnosis.* New York: Brunner/Mazel.

Lankton, S. R., & Lankton, C. H. (1989). *Tales of enchantment.* New York: Brunner/Mazel.

Lazarus, R. (1979). Positive denial: The case for not facing reality. *Psychology Today, 13*(6), 44–60.

Lazarus, A. (1984). *In the mind's eye: The power of imagery for personal enrichment.* New York: Guilford.

Leary, D. E. (Ed.) (1990). *Metaphors in the history of psychology.* Cambridge, England: Cambridge University Press.

Levinson, A. (1978). *The seasons of a man's life.* New York: Knopf.

Lockard, J. S., & Paulhus, D. L. (Eds.) (1988). *Self-deception: An adaptive mechanism.* Englewood Cliffs, NJ: Prentice-Hall.

Lovaas, O. I., Koegel, R. L., & Schreibman, L. (1979). Stimulus overselectivity in autism: A review of research. *Psychological Bulletin, 86*, 1236–1254.

Lozanov, G. (1978). *Suggestology and outlines of suggestopedy.* New York: Gordon & Breach.

Luks, A. (1988). Helper's high. *Psychology Today, 22*(10), 39–42.

MacCormac, E. R. (1985). *A cognitive theory of metaphor.* Cambridge, MA: MIT Press.

Maddi, S., & Kosaba, S. (1984). *The hardy executive: Health under stress.* Homewood, IL: Dow Jones–Irwin.

Maher, B. A. (1966). *Principles of psychopathology: An experimental approach.* New York: McGraw-Hill.

Maher, B. A. (1983). A tentative theory of schizophrenic utterance. In B. A. Maher & W. Maher (Eds.), *Progress in experimental personality research* (Vol. 12, pp. 1–52). Orlando, FL: Academic.

Mahler, M., Pine, F., & Berman, A. (1975). *The psychological birth of the human infant: Symbiosis and individuation.* New York: Basic.

Mahoney, M. J. (1991). *Human change processes: The scientific foundations of psychotherapy.* New York: Basic.

Mahoney, M. J., Gabriel, T. J., & Perkins, T. S. (1987). Psychological skills and exceptional athletic performance. *Sport Psychologist, 1,* 181–199.

Marmot, M. G., & Syme, S. L. (1976). Acculturation and coronary heart disease in Japanese-Americans. *American Journal of Epidemiology, 104,* 225–247.

Marmot, M. G., Syme, S. L., Kagan, A., Kats, H., Cohen, J. B., & Belsky, J. (1975). Epidemiological studies of coronary heart disease and stroke in Japanese men living in Japan, Hawaii and California: Prevalence of coronary hypertensive heart disease and associated risk factors. *American Journal of Epidemiology, 102,* 514–525.

Maslow, A. H. (1975). Lessons from peak-experiences. In A. Arkoff (Ed.), *Psychology and personal growth* (pp. 210–216). Boston: Allyn & Bacon.

Masters, R. E. L., & Houston, J. (1966). *The varieties of psychedelic experience.* New York: Delta.

Masters, R. E. L., & Houston, J. (1972). *Mind games.* New York: Delta.

Mathews, A., May, J., Mogg, K., & Eysenck, M. (1990). Attentional bias in anxiety: Selective search or defective filtering? *Journal of Abnormal Psychology, 99,* 166–173.

Matthews, W. J., & Dardeck, K. L. (1985). Construction of metaphor in the counseling process. *American Mental Health Counselors Association Journal, 7,* 11–23.

Maxeiner, J. (1987). Concentration and distribution of attention in sport. *International Journal of Sports Psychology, 18,* 247–255.

McKechnie, A. A., Wilson, F., Watson, N., & Scott, D. (1983). Anxiety states: A preliminary report on the value of connective tissue massage. *Journal of Psychosomatic Research, 27,* 125–129.

Melges, F. T. (1982). *Time and the inner future: A temporal approach to psychiatric disorders.* New York: Wiley.

Mills, J. C., & Crowley, R. J. (1986). *Therapeutic metaphors for children and the child within.* New York: Brunner/Mazel.

Naranjo, C., & Ornstein, R. E. (1971). *On the psychology of meditation.* New York: Viking.

Nesse, R. M. (1991). What good is feeling bad? *The Sciences, 3*(6), 30–37.

Nesser, U. (1976). *Cognition and reality.* San Francisco: Freeman.

Nettleton, B. (1986). Flexibility of attention and elite athletes' performance in "fast-ball-games." *Perceptual and Motor Skills, 63,* 991–994.

Nideffer, R. M. (1986). Concentration and attention control training. In J. M. Williams (Ed.), *Applied sports psychology: Personal growth to peak experience* (pp. 258– 259). Palo Alto, CA: Mayfield.

Norman, D. A. (1969). *Memory and attention: An introduction to human information processing.* New York: Wiley.

Novak, M. (1978). *The experience of nothingness.* New York: Harper Torchbooks.

O'Hanlon, B. (1986). The use of metaphor for treating somatic complaints in psychotherapy. *Family Therapy Collections, 19,* 19–24.

O'Hanlon, W. H. (1987). *Taproots: Underlying principles of Milton Erickson's therapy and hypnosis.* New York: Norton.

O'Hanlon, W. H., & Hexum, A. L. (1990). *An uncommon casebook: The complete clinical work of Milton H. Erickson, M.D.* New York: Norton.

Ornstein, R. (1986). *The psychology of consciousness* (3rd ed.). New York: Penguin.

Ornstein, R. (1989). *Multiminds.* Garden City, NY: Anchor.

Ornstein, R., & Ehrlich, P. (1989). *New world, new mind.* New York: Touchstone.

Ornstein, R., & Sobel, D. (1987). *The healing brain.* New York: Simon & Schuster.

Ornstein, R., & Sobel, D. (1989). *Healthy pleasures.* Reading, MA: Addison-Wesley.

Ortony, A. (1979). *Metaphor and thought.* Cambridge, England: Cambridge University Press.

Padgett, W. P., & Hill, A. K. (1989). Maximizing athletic performance in endurance events: A comparison of cognitive strategies. *Journal of Applied Social Psychology, 19,* 331–340.

Pekala, R. J. (1982). *The Phenomenology of Consciousness Inventory (PCI).* Thorndale, PA: Phenomenological Concepts.

Pekala, R. J., & Kumar, V. K. (1988). Phenomenological variations in attention across low, medium, and high susceptible subjects. *Imagination, Cognition and Personality, 7*, 303– 314.

Perls, F. S. (1947). *Ego, hunger and aggression: A revision of Freud's theory and method.* New York: Random House.

Peterson, C., & Bossio, L. M. (1991). *Health and optimism.* New York: Macmillan.

Phares, E. J. (1976). *Locus of control in personality.* Morristown, NJ: General Learning Press.

Progoff, I. (Trans.) (1957). *The cloud of unknowing.* New York: Delta.

Rahula, W. (1959). *What the Buddha taught.* New York: Grove.

Redding, R. E. (1990). Metacognitive instruction: Trainers teaching thinking skills. *Performance Improvement Quarterly, 3*, 27–41.

Rich, A. R., & Woolever, D. K. (1988). Expectancy and self-focused attention: Experimental support for the self-regulation model of test anxiety. *Journal of Social and Clinical Psychology, 7*, 246–259.

Rider, M. S., & Achterberg, J. (1989). The effect of music-meditated imagery on neutrophils and lymphocytes. *Biofeedback and Self-Regulation, 14*, 247–257.

Rider, M. S., Achterberg, J., Lawlis, G. F., Goven, A., Toledo, R., & Butler, J. R. (1990). Effect of immune system imagery on secretory IgA. *Biofeedback and Self-Regulation, 15*, 317–333.

Rosen, S. (1982). *My voice will go with you: The teaching tales of Milton H. Erickson.* New York: Norton.

Rossi, E. L. (Ed.) (1980). *The collected papers of Milton H. Erickson on hypnosis.* New York: Irvington.

Rossi, E. L. (1986). *The psychobiology of mind–body healing: New concepts in therapeutic hypnosis.* New York: Norton.

Russell, W. (1979). *Second wind.* New York: Random House.

St. John of the Cross (1953). *The complete works of St. John of the Cross.* Westminster, England: Newman.

Samuel, A. L. (1959). Some studies in machine learning using the game of checkers. *IBM Journal of Research and Development, 3*, 210–229.

Samuels, M., & Bennett, H. (1974). *Spirit guides: Access to inner worlds.* New York: Random House.

Schaefer, C., Coyne, J. C., & Lazarus, R. S. (1981). The health-related functions of social support. *Journal of Behavioral Medicine, 4,* 381–406.

Schier, M. F., & Carver, C. S. (1985). Optimism, coping and health: Assessment and implications of generalized outcome expectancies. *Journal of Personality, 55,* 169–210.

Seligman, M. E. P. (1990). *Learned optimism.* New York: Knopf.

Shapiro, D. (1980). *Meditation: Self-regulation strategy and altered state of consciousness.* New York: Aldine.

Simonton, O. C., & Matthews-Simonton, S. (1978). *Getting well again.* New York: Tarchese.

Smilkstein, G. (1988). Health benefits of helping patients cope. *Consultant, 6,* 56–67.

Smith, C. W., Schneider, J., Minning, C., & Whitcher, S. (1983). Imagery and neutrophil function studies: A preliminary report. Unpublished manuscript, Michigan State University, East Lansing.

Sullivan, H. S. (1953). *The interpersonal theory of psychiatry.* New York: Norton.

Surrey, J. (1991). The "self-in-relation": A theory of women's development. In J. Jordan, D. Kaplan, J. Baher-Miller, I. Stinis, & J. Surrey (Eds.), *Women's growth in connection* (pp. 51–66). New York: Guilford.

Svenson, O. (1981). Are we all less risky and more skillful than our fellow drivers? *Acta Psychologica, 47,* 143–148.

Tart, C. T., & Deikman, A. (1991). Mindfulness, spiritual seeking and psychotherapy. *Journal of Transpersonal Psychology, 23,* 29–52.

Taylor, S. E. (1989). *Positive illusions.* New York: Basic.

Taylor, S. E., & Crocker, J. (1981). Schematic bases of social information processing. In E. T. Higgins, C. P. Herman, & M. P. Zanna (Eds.), *Social cognition: The Ontario symposium* (Vol. 1, pp. 89–135). Hillsdale, NJ: Erlbaum.

Underwood, G. (1976). *Attention and memory.* New York: Pergamon.

Vernon, P. E. (Ed.) (1970). *Creativity.* Middlesex, England: Penguin.

Wall, T. W. (1991). Ethics—the royal road to legitimacy. *American Journal of Clinical Hypnosis, 34,* 73–78.

Wallace, R. K., & Benson, H. (1972). The physiology of meditation. *Scientific American, 226,* 85–90.

Wallston, K. A., & Wallston, B. S. (1982). Who is responsible for your health? The construct of health locus of control. In G. Saunders & J. Sols (Eds.), *Social psychology of health and illness* (pp. 65–95). Hillsdale, NJ: Erlbaum.

Walters, C. (1988a, March). So needy, so nurturant: A feminist therapist looks at popular psychology's view of women. Paper presented at the National Association for Women in Psychology, Bethesda.

Walters, C. (1988b, December). Unconsciousness raising: Utilizing Ericksonian techniques to promote feminist perspectives. Workshop presented at third International Congress on Ericksonian Approaches to Hypnotherapy and Psychotherapy, San Francisco.

Warm, J. S. (Ed.) (1984). *Sustained attention in human performance.* New York: Wiley.

Watts, A. (1957). *The way of Zen.* New York: Pantheon.

Weitzenhoffer, A. M. (1953). *Hypnotism: An objective study in suggestibility.* New York: Wiley.

Welch, M. J. (1984). Using metaphor in psychotherapy. *Journal of Psychosocial Nursing and Mental Health Services, 22,* 13–18.

White, J. (Ed.) (1972). *The highest state of consciousness.* New York: Aldine-Atherton.

White, J. (1974). *What is meditation?* New York: Anchor.

Williams, R. (1989). *The trusting heart: Great news about type A behavior.* New York: Random House.

Williams, S., Kinney, P., & Falbo, J. (1989). Generalization of therapeutic changes in agoraphobia: The role of perceived self-efficacy. *Journal of Consulting and Clinical Psychology, 57,* 436–442.

Wolinsky, S., & Ryan, M. O. (1991). *Trances people live: Healing approaches in quantum psychology.* Sheffield, MA: Bramble.

Wolpe, J. (1969). *The practice of behavior therapy.* New York: Pergamon.

Wrisberg, C. A., & Pein, R. L. (1990). Past running experience as a mediator of the attentional focus of male and female recreational runners. *Perceptual and Motor Skills, 70,* 427–432.

Wurtman, J. (1986). *Managing your mind and mood through food.* New York: Rawson.

Yalom, I. D. (1975). *The theory and practice of group psychotherapy* (2nd ed.). New York: Basic.

Zeig, J. K. (1980). *A teaching seminar with Milton H. Erickson.* New York: Brunner/Mazel.

Zeig, J. K. (1988). An Ericksonian phenomenological approach to therapeutic hypnotic induction and symptom utilization. In J. K. Zeig & S. R. Lankton (Eds.), *Developing Ericksonian therapy: State of the art* (pp. 353–375). New York: Brunner/Mazel.

Zeig, J. K., & Geary, B. B. (1990). Seeds of strategic and interactional psychotherapies: Seminal contributions of Milton H. Erickson. *American Journal of Clinical Hypnosis, 33*, 105–112.

AUTHOR INDEX

SUBJECT INDEX